Moses:CEO

Also by Robert L. Dilenschneider

Power and Influence: Mastering the Art of Persuasion

*A Briefing for Leaders: Communications as the
Ultimate Exercise of Power*

On Power

The Critical 14 Years of Your Professional Life

Moses : CEO

LESSONS
IN LEADERSHIP

by
Robert L. Dilenschneider

New Millennium Press

ISBN 1-893224-02-3

Printed in the United States of America

New Millennium Press
a division of New Millennium Entertainment
350 S. Beverly Drive
Suite 315
Beverly Hills, California 90212

10 9 8 7 6 5 4 3 2 1

To my brother, Jack,
who leads people through quiet resolve
and obvious example

Contents

Acknowledgments   ix

Preface   xi

Introduction: Moses as Everyman   1

1 More Than Mortal?   9

2 Leaders Must Follow   27

3 Humility   43

4 Self-control   65

5 Gratitude   89

6 Justice and Compassion   105

7 Being the Critic   121

8 In Hard Times   145

9 No Spin Doctors   161

Summary   175

Acknowledgments

This book is quite different from *The Critical 14 Years of Your Professional Life,* which I authored two years ago. At that time, I was focusing on young people. Today, however, I am focusing on individuals across the age spectrum.

We have come to think of the corporate CEO as emblematic of leadership. But I believe that many more of us have a genuine capacity for meaningful leadership, often untapped, in most aspects of our lives—whether professional or personal.

Of all the illustrious figures who have graced the human historical record, I discovered—quite unexpectedly—a veritable cornucopia of invaluable leadership lessons in the life, times, and writings of the greatest of the Hebrew prophets—Moses. Thus, the title and theme of this book.

This book would not have been possible without the support of so many people:

My wife, Jan, and our sons, Geoffrey and Peter, were generous with their time and helped me formulate many of the ideas presented here.

Reid Boates, my agent, continually supports my various writing projects.

Mary Jane Genova helped conceptualize the ideas, conduct the research, and prepare the manuscript. I, particularly, am in her debt.

Rabbi Arthur Schneier provided encouragement and insights into what really happened and I am truly in his debt.

At New Millennium Press, Michael Viner, my long-time friend, gave me the opportunity to write and publish the book and I will always be in his debt. Shelly Kale, one of the best editors I have worked with, provided the direction and the necessary comments to ensure the book's completion. Anita Keys, production manager, and Jeffrey Cohen, designer, brought about the book's production.

At The Dilenschneider Group, John Kasic provided his usual superb technical support; Joel Pomerantz gave of his time and abilities to pull the pieces together; and Joan Avagliano ensured it all came together in a timely way.

Preface

—

Why Moses? The story of the biblical leader is one of courage, faith, passion, and determination. These are the defining characteristics of a great hero. They're also the same qualities that have guided leaders throughout history: Mahatma Gandhi, Mother Teresa, Martin Luther King Jr. And they're the qualities that can make anyone a leader—even in today's fast-paced world.

For more than thirty-two hundred years, Moses' saga has stood as one of our greatest examples of leadership. Yet his humble beginnings might have indicated otherwise. The son of Hebrew slaves, Moses wasn't born into a family business, nor did he inherit wealth or power. By great fortune, he escaped his fate— and that of every newborn male Hebrew baby—of being drowned in the river Nile, and he reached manhood as a member of the Pharaoh's family. The story is well known: how he was cast out of Egypt, found a home in the desert with a Midianite tribe, and ultimately became a leader of his people.

Perhaps for the onetime privileged Egyptian prince, tending sheep in the desert with the Midianites was lonely, menial work. Having been schooled by Egypt's best court tutors, Moses may have felt overqualified for the job, not unlike many of today's college graduates who begin their professional lives in the mail room or another entry-level position. But Moses was called on to undertake a difficult, seemingly impossible role: to guide his people out of Egypt and to the Promised Land. Like many leaders, he was thrust into this position, and not always under the most favorable circumstances.

Leadership often comes at times of crisis, frustration, or hardship, when the need for change is pressing. Although many of today's leaders find their opportunities served up by way of more conventional means, the call to assume control of one's destiny is seldom predictable.

After Candy Lightner's thirteen-year-old daughter was killed by a drunk hit-and-run driver in 1980, the wife and mother founded Mothers Against Drunk Drivers (MADD), an organization that now flourishes in six hundred chapters with nearly three million members. William Edward Burghardt Du Bois, the first African American to earn a doctorate degree from Harvard University, recoiled at the treatment of blacks in America and led the movement that resulted in the formation in 1909 of the National Association for the Advancement of Colored People (NAACP). Committed to ensuring the political, educational, social, and economic equality of minorities, the NAACP today has a membership of more than half a million.

Not all leaders approach their role with confidence or the certainty of success. Moses tried to talk God out of assigning him his task. He questioned his own ability to perform. Like most people who are faced with great responsibility, Moses doubted his own strengths while realizing his weaknesses.

Today's leaders often feel just as Moses did—inadequately prepared for the seemingly overwhelming challenges. Moses argued with God, suggesting that he wasn't up to the task physically and lacked the emotional commitment. According to the story, he spoke to God before the Burning Bush, providing numerous excuses as to why he was an inappropriate candidate for the job, from lack of eloquence to being slow of speech. But the Lord would not be convinced. At that moment in the wilderness, Moses' style of leadership was born, reluctantly and with great trepidation.

So too is it with many of those who must push past their personal insecurities to climb the mountain of success. Learning how to overcome those insecurities and achieve one's goals are universal aspects of effective leadership. Through doubt come questions, and through questions come answers.

By the time Moses led the Israelites out of Egypt, he had understood all the prerequisites for effective leadership and acquired most of them. He had a cause—leading his people to the Promised Land. He had passion—God had instilled in him the faith to pursue his goal. He had intelligence—and used it to develop wisdom. And he had determination—albeit determination laced with occasional self-doubt and anxiety. Like all of humankind, Moses was far from perfect, but with these prerequisites, and despite the odds, he was in a position to become a superlative leader.

Ultimately, Moses became a great leader, and he passed on his wisdom to his followers. It is a wisdom that has not been diminished by the ages, nor is it by any means out of step with our own times. If anything, Moses' example transcends time, providing today's men and women with sure guideposts for becoming effective leaders. Far more than just a tale of a man who motivated thousands of slaves to find freedom, Moses' story reveals the basic elements of successful leadership skills and how to obtain them.

Introduction

==

Moses as Everyman

The Moses of the Bible is, in some respects, an Everyman. That's because many leaders share Moses' strengths and weaknesses: his insights and his blind spots, his hopes and his nightmares. Socrates, Jesus, Queen Elizabeth I, Peter the Great, Pope John XXIII, Joan of Arc—all were Moses. Today Moses lives in the United Nations, in the United States Senate, among the Buddhists, and in the poorest parts of Brazil.

Aren't we all leaders at some time in our lives? Maybe we never ran for Congress. Maybe we were never bosses. Few of us headed a major religion. But haven't we been leaders if we've been parents? If we were editors of the school newspaper or captains of the tennis team? If we ran a small business? Or if we led the drive to raise funds for the local firehouse?

We might have been the ones to speak up about the need for a traffic light on our street, or to push for better schools. That means we were leaders. We have taken responsibility for making the world a better place.

Every store manager who has to motivate a staff to generate sales, every teacher who is called on to inspire a student, every department head who is expected to unify a team—all are leaders. Regardless of our role in society or our job in the marketplace, every one of us has the ability to be a leader.

The Universals of Leadership

Leadership in Moses' time wasn't much different than it is today. Sure, Moses didn't have to contend with the media, and nobody was checking his tax returns. But he did encounter many of the same problems that leaders experience today.

- Moses' people were scared. The more frightened they became, the more they back-bit and challenged his leadership. At times they actually wanted to kill him. Today, in a time of economic uncertainty and rapid change, who among us isn't scared? Perhaps that's one reason why we've become so hard on our leaders.

- Moses didn't feel he had the right skills. He felt inadequate. Yet the Lord pushed him to lead the Israelites from Egypt to the Promised Land. He didn't let Moses off the hook. Today people say they aren't going to run for public office because they can't stand up to all the investigation by the media and the taunts of enemies. They say they can't take over a global business because they don't have enough international experience. They say they can't be good parents because their own parents were poor role models. Many of these people don't get off the hook, however. Like Moses, they have to serve as leaders despite their weaknesses. And just like Moses, they usually blossom.

- Moses served two masters. He served his Lord, and as all leaders do, he served or followed the wishes of his people. Good luck with this balancing act! Today's leaders are torn by the conflicting demands that are placed on them. The shareholders want one thing and the employees want another. Their boss wants all their time and their kids want to see them more. News anchors on television want to present the news accurately, but they also have to worry about ratings.

- Moses juggled justice and compassion. Sometimes he was firm with the rebellious Israelites, sometimes he excused their behavior and pleaded with the Lord not to punish them. Modern leaders also face difficult decisions. District attorneys, Supreme Court justices, the president, even jurors—all are confronted with the decisions involved in seeking the death penalty, sentencing, and considering clemency. It's difficult to constantly balance justice with compassion.

- Moses made mistakes and learned to live with them. Today's leaders also are making their fair share of mistakes. When he was CEO at Sunbeam Corp., Al Dunlap decided to put the company through a radical transformation. His plan proved to be a mistake, and he was forced out. Bill Clinton has had to deal with the aftermath of the Monica Lewinsky sex scandal. Both men had to go on with their lives. Since many of us are now living into our eighties and beyond, moving on after our mistakes is becoming a major challenge.

Putting It in Perspective

By looking at these and other issues in Moses' life, we can gain a perspective on what leadership is today. We can learn how to be an effective leader.

At this time in history, we need that perspective. Around the world we are making fundamental decisions. What brand of capitalism should we advocate? Should families be allowed to have as many children as they desire? Like communism, has liberalism or conservatism proved to be an ideology that hasn't worked? What steps can we take to help societies agree on ethical standards of behavior toward their citizens, despite their type of government? Should we no longer be our brother's keeper?

Moses is an excellent model for us because he was all too human. Moses was a superb leader, but he was never Superman. And given the challenges they face today, few leaders turn out to be supermen or superwomen. Will the company's CEO continue to increase revenue? Will the congresswoman always push through the legislation that her constituents demand?

Where Are All the Leaders Going?

Because there is so much criticism of leaders who are less than perfect, and in light of all the mudslinging that characterizes modern politics, many people have questioned whether they want to continue in their leadership roles. In 1968 President Lyndon Johnson chose not to seek reelection, even though he still had a strong showing in the campaign polls. In the aftermath of the Gulf War, General Colin Powell resisted the urgings of his followers to seek the presidency. So have many other leaders. How can we help them to continue leading?

The Realities of Leadership

Telling the Truth

Fallibility is just one reality both leaders and followers have to wrestle with. Another brutal reality is that leaders are expected to tell the truth, even if the truth doesn't prove popular. In this age of total disclosure, most of us have learned to discern who's telling the truth and who isn't. Ironically, careers have become casualties of the truth.

During the 1984 presidential race, Democratic candidate Walter Mondale supported raising taxes in order to reduce budget deficits. His opponent, Ronald Reagan, championed the more popular "no more taxes" platform. Mondale lost the election, and the Reagan administration went on to create the biggest deficit in the country's history. Mondale may have been right, but telling the truth cost him the election.

Moses was truthful about how he felt when the Israelites fashioned the golden calf. He took a stand and broke the tablets containing the Ten Commandments. Perhaps by studying how Moses handled truth, we can learn what level of candor is expected from leaders.

Selflessness

Another issue is selflessness. In this age of celebrity, leaders tend to get a lot of attention. Back in Moses' time, however, it was easier for leaders to be selfless. Moses put his people before himself. When he was dying, he was more concerned about comforting the Israelites than about personally entering the Promised Land or even having an easy death. Is it possible for a leader in the twenty-first century to be this selfless?

Followership

There is also the concept of "followership." Throughout our lives we are called on to be both leaders and followers. Yet few of us learn how to become good followers. When we're growing up, we're not encouraged to become excellent followers. I have yet to come across a college application that asks for evidence of followership. Like Moses, we must learn to be astute and dedicated followers if we want to become astute and dedicated leaders. Moses shows us how to balance leadership with followership.

Moses Today

Let us indulge our imagination for a moment: If Moses were to come back today, might he fancy transforming himself into the writer Gail Sheehy? She is showing the seventy-six million baby boomers in America who are nearing fifty years of age how to grow older with purpose and dignity. Already she has produced three books on aging, all of which are well documented and upbeat. Like Moses, Sheehy keeps growing in knowledge and wisdom.

Or might Moses also come back as Federal Reserve Chairman Alan Greenspan? By controlling our interest rates, Greenspan has dictated our economic destiny. He has tried to be fair. Just as Moses proceeded very carefully, every move on Greenspan's part has been well thought out.

You'll want to read this book if:

- You're considering a leadership role.

- As a leader, you're experiencing burnout and wondering if it's possible to recharge your batteries.

- Everyone tells you that you're a natural leader, but you disagree.

- You're happy being a follower.

- You need to grow spiritually.

- You think you expect too much from your leaders.

- You want more meaning in your life.

**This is a book
for leaders, followers,
and those trying
to become better
human beings.**

1

═══

More Than Mortal?

> One morning a man got out of bed, poured a cup of coffee, and began reading the newspaper. He received quite a shock: on the obituary page of the newspaper, mistakenly, was his own obituary! Equally disturbing to the man was reading about himself solely as someone who had spent his life making weapons of war.
>
> That day the man decided to change his life. He decided to devote his remaining years to world peace and the betterment of humanity. That man was Alfred B. Nobel, founder of the Nobel Prize.

Some of us change the world. Often those of us who make a difference start out as ordinary people. Moses seemed to be an ordinary man—a mere herdsman—until he was called by the Lord to lead the Israelites to the Promised Land. Then he became Moses the leader. He could do things lesser mortals could not.

Starting Out Ordinary

Many of our great leaders were ordinary people who become extraordinary when pushed into particular roles. President Franklin Delano Roosevelt was a beloved and powerful man who brought the country out of the Depression. When he died in office in 1945, Vice President Harry Truman had to step into his shoes. He had to lead the nation through the end of World War II and the beginning of the Cold War.

Truman rose to the occasion. His decision to drop the atomic bomb on Hiroshima and Nagasaki ended the war in the Pacific theater. But he didn't stop there: he worked to rebuild Europe at the end of the war with the implementation of the Marshall Plan in 1948 and to counteract the spread of Soviet imperialism with the formation of NATO in 1949.

When we try to make a difference, we bring out the best in ourselves. Before Malcolm X became concerned about the plight of African Americans, he was just another hardened prison inmate. Once he raised his consciousness about his identity, he became a civil rights leader who helped bring about changes in society's attitude toward blacks.

Thinking of Others

The miracle about making a difference is that while we're doing it, we're not thinking about ourselves. We're getting past our petty, ordinary human concerns. We're not worrying about our mortgage or our weight. Mother Teresa probably was not thinking about getting older—or worrying about her health—when she was working with the desperately poor in Calcutta.

Moses was a reluctant leader. His life was fine as it was. After slaying an Egyptian who was abusing an Israelite, Moses fled. On the way to where he thought he should go, he stopped at a well to help some women draw water for their flocks. He wound up marrying one of them. He and his wife had children. He got along well with his in-laws. This is about all most people want in life. Moses had only himself, his wife, and his family to think about. When he accepted the Lord's mission to lead thousands of men, women, and children, plus livestock, from Egypt to the Land of Milk and Honey, he had a lot more on his plate. He couldn't think only about himself.

It is said that when Lee Iacocca was at the Ford Motor Co. he was not a well-liked man. He was arrogant. Henry Ford II fired him. But when Iacocca was trying to save Chrysler Motors Corp. and the jobs of more than sixty thousand men and women, he could persuade anyone to do anything he needed. He put his career on the line and became a folk hero and a symbol of what was right about American business. Iacocca was able to transcend his ego. His years at Chrysler were the happiest of his life.

From Clark Kent to Superman

When the Lord called on Moses to lead his people, Moses gave the Lord all the reasons why he wasn't the right person for the job. But the Lord wouldn't take no for an answer, and Moses was inducted as a leader. This happens to many people who end up making a difference. They're drafted to serve. And they change.

Look at the history of the United States Supreme Court. Once people are called to serve on the Court, they become very different. Supreme Court Justice Hugo Black was a Klansman in his youth. After he was appointed to the Court, he became a great defender of the first Amendment and a proponent of desegregation. Justice Harry Blackmun was a conservative Midwestern judge who went on to become a spokesman for reproductive choice, the abolition of the death penalty, and other liberal causes.

At many businesses when the No. 2 person becomes No. 1, he or she blossoms. John Welch Jr., CEO of General Electric Corp., wasn't always referred to in management books as America's greatest executive. In 1961, as a junior engineer who had worked at GE for a little more than a year, Welch was offered a standard $1,000 raise to his $10,500 annual salary. The young employee was insulted. Feeling stifled by what he saw as company bureaucracy, he pursued a job at another company. He told his superior at GE about the new offer, and his boss encouraged him to stay and grow with the company. Welch's boss recognized greatness within Welch and successfully cut through the bureaucratic maze to keep him with the firm. For the next twelve years, Welch fulfilled his potential and discovered his cause: ridding GE of the same big-business bureaucracy he had hated as a new recruit. Because of this, GE is a bigger and better company.

Put to the Test

Like most leaders, Moses was put through a series of tests. The Lord sent him to plead with the Pharaoh of Egypt to release the Hebrew slaves, but then hardened the Pharaoh's heart against the Jews. That made Moses' work all the more difficult and frustrating. But he got the job done, and the Israelites left Egypt. These sorts of initial tests are often a rite of passage. If the individual can get past them, then he or she has won the right to be a leader and also has earned the confidence of his or her followers.

In today's volatile global economic environment, we're often tested at work. We lose a job. The boss is mean. We don't get that promotion. The company piles too much work on us. Those of us who pass these tests may emerge as new managers or CEOs.

- Like other automobile industry leaders, executives at General Motors' Saturn division were facing mounting criticism both inside and outside the industry for keeping women and minority employees from top management positions. Confronted with both a shrinking small-car market and damage to its once stellar labor relations, GM appointed Cynthia M. Trudell, an expert on sport utility vehicles and factory management, as chair and president of its Saturn division. GM executives passed the test: they have become leaders in the auto industry's challenge to break the glass ceiling for qualified women executives.

- Olympic speed skater Dan Jansen underwent a series of tests before finally winning the gold medal at the 1994 Winter Olympics in Lillehammer, Norway. Ten years earlier, in 1984, he missed winning the bronze medal by only hundredths of a second. Four years later, in 1988, stronger and more determined, he competed in the Winter Olympics in Calgary, Canada. On the day he was to compete in the 500-meter race, his sister died of leukemia. Only one hundred meters into the race, Jansen stumbled and fell. Had Jansen not endured, had he not passed the test of courage and determination, he would not be a gold medalist today. His success led him to create the Dan Jansen Foundation, an organization that supports programs for education, youth sports, and leukemia research.

- In 1956 John F. Kennedy was passed over for the Democratic vice presidential spot on the Adlai Stevenson ticket. The loss didn't keep him from pursuing his dream to serve his country, however. Four years later, he went on to win the presidential race. Had he not faced the challenge of defeat, he might never have gone on to run for president.

> ## Being tested prepares us to lead.

Who Gets the Credit?

Good things often happen to those on a mission.

- Mao Tse-tung organized a small band of guerrilla fighters to resist the Japanese takeover of China in the 1930s. His mission to protect the autonomy of his country led to his rise among his people as a leader and—despite his controversial career—to the unification of China into a powerful nation-state for the first time in its history.

- During the Depression years, Dorothea Lange photographed the plight of poor farmworkers. Her famous portrait, *Migrant Mother,* taken in a pea-picking camp in Nipomo, California, not only cemented her reputation as a leading photographer of social causes but also resulted in the government sending twenty thousand pounds of food supplies to the poverty-stricken workers.

Leaders usually don't take the credit for the good things that happen. Many are selfless.

- When the Egyptians changed their minds and tried to forcibly bring the Israelites back to captivity, the Lord helped out. He parted the Red Sea and the Israelites escaped. Moses was clear that this was the Lord's doing and not his own. He acknowledged the role of the Lord in the Israelites' flight from Egypt and won credibility from his people.

- In Chula Vista, California, Jenny Murphy, a homemaker, has collected supplies for the poor in Mexico. When there is a windfall of support, Murphy always has viewed the good fortune as the result of divine intervention, not her own doing.

- William Hewlett and David Packard of Hewlett Packard walked the floor of their computer-manufacturing plant to hear employees' suggestions and complaints. They allowed the employees to have a voice in helping to make the company more productive and gave them credit for their contributions.

Many top-performing companies issue stock options to their team of workers. The leaders of these corporations truly believe that it is the team, not just themselves, who brings home the bacon.

The Ultimate Risk

Making a difference can cost us our lives. Moses' mission was life-threatening, and he knew it. The Israelites were quick to panic in the desert when there weren't enough supplies or when they saw an enemy army in the distance. They vented their anger at Moses, who had reassured them when they were slaves in Egypt that it was right to leave Egypt. Often they expressed a desire to return to Egypt instead of heading to the Promised Land, but Moses convinced them that there was no going back. Still, they were unnerved. Would they die in the desert? At times they would have stoned Moses had he and the Lord not placated them.

Putting one's life on the line seems to come with the territory of making a difference. The Reverend Martin Luther King Jr.'s civil rights platform brought criticism from both those opposed to racial equality and from more militant African Americans. King feared in his bones that he eventually would be killed for preaching his gospel of passive resistance. Robert Kennedy was aware he had many enemies. At times he seemed to sense that his liberal views might cost him his life. Many Christian missionaries in developing countries frequently risk being massacred.

But the fear of death usually doesn't deter those who are bent on changing the world. They're too busy.

For more than a decade, Aung San Suu Kyi has risked her life and freedom for the establishment of a democratic government in Myanmar (Burma). As co-founder and general secretary of the National League for Democracy, she has spent many years under house arrest and isolation for her role as a leader of the pro-democracy movement. A powerful symbol of heroism and commitment to her ideals, she has become a source of contention to Burma's oppressive military regime. In 1991 she was awarded the Nobel Peace Prize.

Did Florence Nightingale lose sleep over the possibility that she might pick up diseases on the battlefield?

There are things worse than death. The worst is *not being able to change things*. When the late Lois Jaffe, a professor of social work at the University of Pittsburgh, was diagnosed with cancer, she threw herself into the cause of making hospital conditions better for cancer patients. She was more concerned about their health than about her own.

War and Peace

Perhaps one of the heaviest burdens for Moses was deciding between war and peace. In some ways he was like President Truman deciding whether to drop the atomic bomb. According to Moses' beliefs, peace was one of the most important values of the community. Peace meant that all creatures on earth, including animals, should cooperate. But peace comes with a price. According to Moses' religion, war was sometimes defensible as a lesser evil. If the Israelites didn't go to war against an enemy, for example, they might lose all their food supplies or the right to worship their Lord.

When it was necessary to enter a war, however, the Israelites weren't naive. They were afraid. Moses had to use masterful public relations strategies to calm them. As he grew as a leader, Moses changed from a man who could barely speak in public to someone who could persuade thousands of people. The stone tablets—the Ten Commandments—that he brought down from Mount Sinai and that he promulgated are forever with us, reaching and inspiring millions.

A Higher Power

It seems that some higher power often gives leaders what they need when they need it. If we trust in something bigger than ourselves, we too can receive this gift. Hildegard of Bingen, the medieval German abbess, composer, playwright, and theologian, claimed that during one of her visions she heard a voice telling her to say and write what she saw and heard. More than fifteen books of her vision, philosophy, and knowledge resulted. Her musical compositions are still recorded today.

Those on a mission often don't care if they themselves will ever reach their goal. What counts is the process of trying to make a difference. The cause is bigger than they are.

Moses had a temper tantrum when he returned from Mount Sinai with the Ten Commandments and saw the Israelites worshiping a golden calf. He threw down the tablets containing the laws for his people and broke them into pieces. Although the Israelites had violated perhaps the most sacred of commandments, that didn't deter him from continuing his mission to lead the Chosen People to the Promised Land. He kept his focus on the job. He loved his people more than himself, and he wanted them to make it.

Nelson Mandela opposed apartheid in South Africa and was imprisoned for his beliefs for twenty-six years. He was offered freedom by the apartheid government rulers in exchange for renouncing his views. But Mandela was strong in his principles. He refused to leave his prison cell until apartheid was abolished. His commitment to the cause of equality was greater than his personal freedom.

Letting Go

Making a difference often means being willing to let go. Moses was ready to give up some of his authority when he thought that the people were able to take care of their spiritual needs. After the tabernacle was completed, the Israelites worshiped their Lord on their own. They had matured spiritually. Moses told the Lord that he would now step aside. The Lord, however, had more spiritual work for Moses to do on behalf of the people— for example, teaching the community the laws regarding what was right and wrong in human behavior.

Wise leaders are prepared to leave the scene when the time comes.

- In 1993 Harvey Golub took over the reins as CEO of American Express. His mandate: to lead the company and its demoralized workforce out of a weakened state brought about by costly forays into brokerage and investment banking services and by the competitive threat of other companies issuing credit and charge cards. Four years later, after substantially raising the company's net income, Golub announced his plans to retire. He designated a successor and a timetable for retirement to prepare the company for the change in command and to eliminate speculation about its future. In 1999 Golub moved up his retirement date by three years. He was able to give up the power and perks of a successful corporate job and hand over the reins to others.

- After winning six NBA championships for his team and being acknowledged as the greatest basketball player of all time, Michael Jordan decided to retire. By recognizing when it was time to leave, Jordan assured himself a place in the history of the game.

- As a student, Tom Hayden was a leader in the antiwar movement and a Chicago Seven defendant during the 1960s and 1970s. In the 1980s he successfully made the transition to electoral politics. He recognized that it was time to give up trying to overthrow the system as a revolutionary leader and work for change from within.

The Test of Time

As a visionary, Moses spoke for all times. His words and deeds have become part of our collective memory. The Lord said that Moses is "faithful in all my House" (Num. 12:7). By this the Lord meant that Moses' counsel was applicable to the House of Israel forever.

Timelessness can be the acid test of leadership: Will the next generation find guidance and comfort in the leader's words and actions?

- Winston Churchill's early and staunch opposition to Adolf Hitler and the spread of Nazism still resonates with today's leaders who fight fascist or other totalitarian regimes.

- Economist John Maynard Keynes's theory on governmental intervention influenced legislators of the New Deal and helped bring the country out of the Depression. Today's economic leaders take Keynes's contributions for granted in formulating the government's response to economic crises.

- Mahatma Gandhi's teachings about nonviolent resistance were adopted by many leaders, including Martin Luther King Jr. Other civil rights leaders as well as proponents of democratic ideals the world over—including such leaders as Poland's Lech Walesa and the Czech Republic's Václav Havel—have heeded his advice.

Those Who Have Shown Us the Way

Fortunately, many people have made a beneficial difference. They didn't always start out to do so, but it happened nevertheless. And they gradually accepted the mantle of leadership.

- George Wallace was a staunch supporter of segregation during the 1960s. In 1972, after an assassination attempt on his life while he was running for the Democratic presidential nomination, Wallace changed his stance. He brought African Americans into his administration as governor of Alabama and became a popular leader with the black community.

- In her testimony in connection with the appointment of Clarence Thomas to the Supreme Court in 1991, Anita Hill accused Thomas of sexual harassment when he was her supervisor at the Equal Employment Opportunity Commission. Hill was initially reluctant to testify before the Senate Judiciary Committee, but she ultimately agreed. Her controversial testimony instigated new inquiries into the laws concerning sexual harassment as they apply to our top political leaders. Today Hill is a leading spokesperson against sexual harassment in the workplace and the corridors of power.

- Brenda Barnes, formerly an executive at Pepsico, took the road less traveled. She left a high-powered job to spend more time with her children. She is an example for the women—and men—today who choose family responsibilities over their careers and find themselves having to stand up to the controversy surrounding their decision.

Those Who Could Have Been Better

Many people have embraced the role of leader, only to fall short of accomplishing their goals.

- O. J. Simpson could have been a powerful role model for African Americans. The former pro football star won the Heisman trophy for best college player, set the record for most yards rushing in a single season in the 1970s, and received a lucrative contract with Hertz Rent-a-Car as the company's promotional star in its advertising campaign. When he was arrested for the murders of his ex-wife, Nicole Simpson, and her friend, Ronald Goldman, he spent more than a year in jail. Although he was subsequently acquitted in the criminal trial, he was found guilty of wrongful death in the civil trial that followed. Now, being a role model is no longer possible for him.

- President Bill Clinton in many ways has been a successful political leader. But his admission to an extramarital affair with a young White House intern and his civil contempt citation for committing perjury in the Paula Jones case have lost him the respect of his colleagues, fellow legislators, and many Americans.

- Executives at Nike made the company logo synonymous with success and personal achievement. However, when it was discovered that Nike's executives were exploiting their workers—many of whom were children—in the company's overseas factories, Americans questioned the company's intent.

How You Can Help

When the late Princess Diana arrived at charity functions, she offered to do whatever the organizers wanted, telling them that she was "theirs" for two hours. In this small way Diana helped raise millions of dollars and an awareness of social, health, environmental, and political concerns. There's plenty we can do, in little ways and big.

✓ Care about Others

A man at a large organization where I worked, whom I'll call Frank, knew how to extend himself to his co-workers. He knew the names of our children. He knew when we had a deadline. He read our body language and could anticipate trouble. Frank made that competitive office a safe place. He helped us all. The amazing thing is that when Frank wasn't simply being a great human being, he was doing his own work well enough to rise rapidly in the company. In today's even more competitive organizations, the Franks of the office can have a huge impact. Nice guys generally don't finish last.

✓ Do Pro Bono Work

Whether you're a law student, a plumber, or a computer expert, you can do pro bono work. That means giving your skills away for free. Public relations people who help out struggling causes, for instance, can accomplish miracles.

Billionaire Ross Perot donated millions of dollars and years of his time to start a third political party dedicated to reducing the national debt and reforming campaign fund-raising practices. Even his opponents have recognized him as a major influence in bringing those issues to the political front in the 1992 presidential election.

The actress Elizabeth Taylor has devoted a considerable amount of her time and money to advancing AIDS research. She has received worldwide recognition for establishing the Elizabeth Taylor AIDS Foundation.

All the money that has been used for scientific research and environmental and social causes over the years never would have been raised if plenty of talented people—both famous and unknown—did not do pro bono work.

✔ Start a Business

The businesses we start create jobs. Henry Ford was a hero not only because he invented the Model T. When Ford launched his car-manufacturing business and paid his workers the then unheard-of wage of five dollars a day, he initiated the beginnings of a middle class. Today's hero is the entrepreneur.

✔ E-mail Your Government Representatives

Public opinion is now a powerful force. You can make a difference by telling your government representatives what you think.

✔ Make House Calls

Before the invention of the telephone, we wandered into each other's houses. Now our houses have become fortresses. To get in you need the code. If we can come together once again as human beings, we will see a softening in how we and others see the world. Visit with a friend. Sit on his or her porch.

Isn't it wonderful
that there are
things in life bigger
than ourselves?

2

Leaders Must Follow

Benjamin Disraeli, the British Prime Minister who helped make England more democratic, was a popular and romantic leader. He was constantly in touch with what was on the minds and in the hearts of the people. He understood the needs and desires of England's blue-collar workers. In 1867 his close association with the working class enabled him to pass the Radical Reform Bill, in which blue collar workers received increased representation in Parliament. Disraeli once observed: "I must follow the people. Am I not their leader?"

Staying connected to the people was only half of Disraeli's challenge. In addition to leading them, he had to follow the desires and orders of Queen Victoria. As a subject of the throne, Disraeli had to keep the monarchy pleased with his performance.

A Balancing Act

Being a leader often means balancing the wants and needs of diverse people and groups. Moses had to follow both the people and the Lord. Often his own life was at stake.

Rather than take the Israelites on a direct route to the Promised Land, God directed Moses to take the long way around via the Red Sea. The route presented many obstacles and hardships, and at times the Hebrews were convinced they were going to die. They complained bitterly: "Is not this the word that we did tell thee in Egypt, saying 'Let us alone, that we may serve the Egyptians'? For it had been better for us to serve the Egyptians, than that we should die in the wilderness" (Exod. 14:12).

The people threatened Moses with desertion. They also threatened his life. Moses had to honor his commitment to God as well as to his people. On his journey to the Promised Land, he had to find a way both to obey his Lord and to lead his people.

The Art of Followership

Until recently, followership wasn't encouraged, at least not openly. Followers were derisively called "sheep," "yes people," and "brown noses." At work, performance reviews were based on signs of leadership, not followership. At home and at school, children were encouraged to stand out as leaders and not to be just followers.

Under the surface, however, most of us are looking for ways to please those we follow: the No. 1 person in the company, our boss, the head of the platoon, the captain of our team. Many of us have tried to learn how to become good followers.

Moses as Follower

We probably can learn the most about the art of followership by observing leaders such as Moses.

Carrying out the orders of the Lord while placating and motivating a rebellious people was difficult. When the Lord told Moses to ask the Pharaoh of Egypt to release the Israelites from their duties as slaves and let them go into the desert to celebrate a religious holiday, he obeyed. However, his request infuriated the Pharaoh, who punished the Israelites by withholding the straw for the edifices they were building. Now, the Israelites not only had to make the bricks, but they also had to gather the straw themselves. Moses saw how distressful this was to his followers. He went to bat for them before the Lord, questioning the effectiveness of these dealings with the Pharaoh.

The Lord told Moses: "Now shalt thou see what I will do to Pharaoh" (Exod. 6:1). The Lord showed Pharaoh his power. Like all good followers, Moses had faith in the Lord, didn't argue his case any further, and encouraged the Israelites also to believe.

When the Israelites were trapped at the Red Sea with the Egyptian soldiers in close pursuit, they panicked. God told Moses to place his shepherd's staff in his right hand and raise it over the Red Sea. Moses obeyed. The waters parted and the Israelites escaped.

In balancing the interests of both the Lord and the people, Moses' trust in the Lord played a major role. By following his leader, Moses empowered the Lord to help the Hebrews achieve their freedom.

Tapping into Resources

As the Israelites moved from the familiarity of Egypt to the unknown expanse of the desert, their anger toward Moses escalated. Sometimes their hostility was threatening to Moses and his brother, Aaron. Moses tried to determine what the Hebrews needed. Maybe they wanted water. Maybe they wanted to feel safe from their enemies.

In this volatile atmosphere, Moses assessed his people's mood. He admitted his fears to himself. Then he reported to the Lord the urgency of the situation.

After crossing the Red Sea, the Israelites' water and food supplies ran low. The people threatened Moses with desertion and worse. But God provided a spring for fresh water and, later, manna to eat. The Lord provided what the people wanted and their anger dissipated.

Leaders who are good followers know where to go to get what they need. Napoleon used to muse that armies marched on their stomachs. He kept his troops well fed.

Asking for Help

Recognizing when to surrender and request help is an art in itself. As a good follower, Moses knew when to ask the Lord for relief from the burden of leadership. When he cried out to the Lord that he no longer could carry the responsibility of guiding the Israelites alone, the Lord helped him design a primitive type of organizational command that relieved him of some of the nuts and bolts of leadership.

Moses' acute awareness of his situation and his willingness to ask for help are exactly what managers in corporations want their subordinates to do: ask for help before there's a catastrophe. This requires just the right timing. Requesting help prematurely can be interpreted as whining. Requesting help after disaster strikes can be perceived as blaming.

Reading the People

Moses knew he had to appeal to what mattered most to the people. He was always studying what made the Israelites tick. Today Moses might have hired a polling firm.

When Moses tried to mobilize the people into battle, he was asked: "Whither shall we go up? Our brethren have discouraged our heart, saying, 'The people is greater and taller than we; the cities are great and walled up to heaven'" (Deut. 1:28).

He responded to the people's fear by telling them what they needed to hear. He reminded them that the Lord was fighting on their side, just as he took care of them in the desert. He reminded them that the Land of Milk and Honey had been promised to them and that, therefore, they had quite a bit at stake in winning the battle. He reminded them that their children, whom they prized, would inherit the Promised Land. By acknowledging the Israelites' fear and addressing it, Moses was able to reach the people, and the people were more willing to comply.

Obeying Orders

In his relationship with the Lord, Moses recognized the importance of obeying the letter of the law. The Lord often could be very literal. If the Lord wanted a tabernacle built to certain dimensions and with certain decorations, Moses guided the Israelites to do exactly that. Ritual was an important part of the Hebrews' religion. If Moses hadn't stuck to the letter of the law in ritualistic activity, the people would have been less unified.

Good followers know intuitively which rules have to be obeyed and which don't. A prized employee in an organization is one who doesn't require much supervision. And, like Moses, a good executive sets fair but explicit rules and insists that they be followed.

Followership Returns

In 1980 Harvard Business School professors John Gabarro and John Kotter made big names for themselves with their classic essay "Managing Your Boss," published in the *Harvard Business Review*. They suggested that followers pay particular attention to their leaders' preferences in both their communication style and decision-making process. Does your boss prefer written memos or informal meetings? Is your leader more intuitive or methodical where decisions are concerned? Followers can help their leaders to lead.

Since the publication of Gabarro and Kotter's essay, articles on followership have appeared in many other business publications, including the *Wall Street Journal*. Although kids aren't yet saying they want to grow up to be followers, we are learning that there are important payoffs in following effectively and being part of a team.

Teamwork

Why is followership being considered seriously? Today professional life demands that people act sometimes as followers and sometimes as leaders. No single person in this information age has all the answers or resources. Usually, only a team of people can attack a problem. Thomas Edison built many of his inventions by himself, but it took a team to put the minivan on the road.

Nearly every day, business newspapers and journals announce more global alliances and joint ventures. This means that entire organizations will be working together. In some of its roles, Corporation A will be a leader because it excels in that area. But in other roles, Corporation A will be a follower, learning from its more experienced partner.

Melding cultures has become one of the most difficult tasks facing business leaders today. When Chrysler Motors Corp. merged with the German automaker Daimler-Benz to form DaimlerChrysler, company leaders tried to create a new team from two different countries. In the immediate aftermath, it was clear that there were cultural clashes and differences in business management techniques. Despite being assured that they were an integral part of the new team, Chrysler workers began to feel they were working solely for a German company. German business practices, different from American, predominated. Chrysler employees started leaving, and the design of new cars and marketing strategies for individual products began to suffer. The company's leaders are paving new ground in their attempt to direct German and American interests toward a common goal.

Today we need to know the direction the team is taking. If our performance reviews indicate that we don't work well with others, we can be fired. One of the men I first reported to, Chris Hauser of Marathon Oil Company, told me I had to be part of his team to succeed. He told me that the success of the company was tied to the success of the team. Nearly every employee in Marathon supported this view. Marathon was one of the great companies of its day.

In our changing world, followership is no longer as taboo as it once was. It is now a word in our professional vocabulary. We can key in *followership* on a search engine on the Internet and come up with many entries.

Management's Changing Role

Today's CEOs are no longer considered omnipotent. They no longer have jobs for life. They're accountable for their actions. They have to follow the wishes of employees, the board of directors, customers, and shareholders. Those leaders who understand how to follow will thrive.

Since 1984 Reuben Mark has successfully helmed Colgate-Palmolive as chair and CEO. Each year the company returned record earnings. Brand-name recognition of Colgate toothpaste, Palmolive soap, Ajax cleanser, and Science Diet pet foods was high. Despite the company's success, however, Mark knew that the highest percentage of earnings was coming from the European and Asian markets. By 1993 United States and Canadian sales of the company's products had plunged 12 percent, and operating profits had dropped 26 percent. Wall Street suddenly turned the spotlight on the CEO. Was he on his way out?

Fortunately, Mark turned to his corporate followers to help him lead the company out of its quagmire. He elevated executive Lois Juliber, a brand-name wizard who had proven her worth at Kraft Foods, to the post of executive vice president and chief operating officer of the developed markets division. Mark gave Juliber full authority to reorganize the company's domestic operations. In three years Colgate-Palmolive had surpassed perennial leader Procter & Gamble as the leading supplier of toothpaste in the world. Mark came off a hero as a result of his ability to follow Juliber's leadership.

With today's worldwide technological, social, and political changes, leadership and followership roles are evolving. It used to be that "father knew best." Now, fathers may look to their children for guidance on how to navigate in the digital world. Even Queen Elizabeth II hires a public relations consultant to help her understand what the people want.

Wise leaders know when to be followers and when to assume the role of leader.

Being an Effective Follower

According to Ira Chaleff, author of *Learn the Art of Followership*, "Follower skills are learned informally, like street fighting." We can learn how to become followers from those who have tried.

- William R. Johnson, CEO of H. J. Heinz Co., has relied on his blunt, down-to-earth management style to lead the company effectively. He has initiated share-ownership rules in order to make his managers "think like owners." He has encouraged open debate among his employees. "I've made it very clear," he has said. "Don't tell me what I think. I know what I think. Tell me what you think."

- Patricia C. Dunn has used her management skills and adaptive mind to run Barclays Global Investors. "Probably the thing that I did at the point of my career where I advanced the most involved helping clients figure out how to use our highly sophisticated investment services to their advantage," she has said. By listening to and following her clients' leads, Dunn has been able to merge successfully the company's technological advancements with the real-life applications that her clients demanded.

- Scudder Kemper Investments Inc. representative Dave Murphy wasn't as successful. When he traveled to Window Rock, Arizona, to meet with employees of the Navajo Nation, he received a valuable lesson in followership. He was unprepared for the economic, cultural, and educational differences between his Native American clients and the employees of other companies he had dealt with previously. The terms he was using to explain the Navajo administration's new retirement plan—*savings, stocks, asset allocation,* and *tax-deferred compounding*—were not easily accepted or understood. Unable to adapt Scudder's teaching methods to their needs, Navajo Nation employees initiated their own lecture series on retirement planning. Headed by a staff member, the series has attracted more employees to the retirement plan. By following the lead of its employees, the Navajo retirement administration has brought more of its staff toward greater financial security.

Those Who Led by Following

Moses was an effective follower. He followed the Lord to Egypt. He followed the Hebrew elders in gaining the support of the Hebrew slaves. He followed the wisdom of his father-in-law, Jethro, in the Midian desert. He closely followed the process of spiritual growth among his people and led them accordingly. Like him, many notable men and women have led by following.

- Saint Francis of Assisi is famous for communing with animals and founding a religious order. He championed poverty and a life of service, taking a secondary position to others in an effort to be a more effective leader.

- The Austrian psychoanalyst Sigmund Freud treated patients who consulted him for a variety of inexplicable conditions, ranging from paralysis to hysteria. By listening to his patients, he developed a revolutionary theory that emphasized unconscious thought and the influence of sexuality on human behavior. His ability to follow his patients' lead enabled him to become a pioneer in understanding the mind-body connection.

- John Sculley was Pepsico's youngest vice president of marketing. His "Pepsi Generation" ad campaign cemented his reputation as a savvy marketing executive who knew how to appeal to young adults. He was lured away from Pepsico by Apple Computer chair and co-founder Steve Jobs to become that company's president. The move from Pepsico to Apple was a big change for Sculley. He had to learn technology. He had to learn an entirely new market. He had to learn how to interact with people whose whole universe was based on electronics. And he did. Deferring to Jobs and his staff, Sculley became a good follower. When he decided that his education was over, he became more of a leader.

- As president of NBC Television, Robert C. Wright faced the challenge of increasing the network's ratings. Rather than issuing his own directives, he built a team of quality advisers around him, and together they developed a plan. His ability to lead by following and being a team member brought the network to new profit highs.

- Pop star and actress Madonna became an international leader of style by following eclectic trends of the past. From Renaissance art to Marilyn Monroe, Madonna found inspiration in a variety of sources and succeeded in using that knowledge to attain a leading position in the entertainment industry. Her chameleon-like ability to reinvent herself again and again has been instrumental in building her multifaceted career.

Those Who Didn't Follow

There are many examples of leaders who could have been greater by learning how to follow. The business community is littered with former CEOs who never figured it out.

- Apple Computer co-founder and chair Steve Jobs drove his workers through grueling hours in his attempt to topple IBM from its No. 1 position in computer sales. He lambasted employees who couldn't keep up the pace. Talented minds burned out before his eyes. Jobs had lost touch with his followers' needs. He wouldn't listen to their problems as he forged ahead in an effort to give birth to the Macintosh personal computer. He was summarily ousted by Apple's president, John Sculley, whom Jobs himself had recruited. When he eventually returned to Apple years later, he was a changed man. He had learned how to follow.

- In the 1992 presidential campaign, President George Bush failed to heed pollsters' warnings that the key issue for most American voters was the poor state of the economy. Perhaps due to his upper-class upbringing, Bush didn't convey that he understood the pain many Americans were feeling as a result of the economic recession. He lost the election to Bill Clinton, whose campaign focus was embodied in his oft-repeated slogan, "It's the economy, stupid."

- Congressman Newt Gingrich rose to the position of Speaker of the House in 1995 after appearing on the national stage in 1978. The first Republican in forty years to hold the position, he was named Man of the Year by *Time* magazine. His blunt and outspoken manner soon alienated many of his followers, however. He seemed to have his own agenda in addition to the one he had promised to uphold in his role as congressional leader. After being forced to give up a $4.5 million advance for two book deals due to charges of conflict of interest, and then being fined for violating House ethics rules by misusing tax-exempt funds, Gingrich lost the votes necessary to maintain the speakership. By failing to embrace his party's agenda, he was unable to lead.

How to Follow

Although learning how to follow might be best accomplished "on the job," some guidelines can help you get ahead of the game.

 Put Others First
The most effective CEOs understand how to be followers. They're able to put aside their egos, their petty concerns, and their biases, and try to meet the needs of the people who matter. Instead of complaining that the stockholders want a 20 percent return on their investment, they go after that goal. When female employees charge that they are being sexually harassed, they launch an investigation.

 Listen
Management consultant Tom Peters (*Thriving on Chaos: Handbook for a Management Revolution*) observed that successful organizations have "listening posts" everywhere. So do leaders.

In the early 1980s, executives of Chrysler Motors Corp. spent more time in the hallways and plants than in their offices in an attempt to turn their nearly bankrupt company around. They discovered that workers already had thought out how to improve the quality of the product they were creating. Whether they worked on the assembly line or in marketing, design, or sales, nearly every employee had an idea. Chrysler's leaders listened. They began making a better automobile. Two years later, Chrysler returned to profitability and repaid its debt seven years early.

Successful leaders know their worth is not diminished by asking for advice and seeking knowledge from others.

 Be Accessible

Scott Adams's cartoon-strip character Dilbert may grouse about his cubicle, but any great leader will tell you it's a gold mine. Everyone can see him and he can see everybody. Dilbert may complain about his lack of privacy, but privacy is a funny commodity. Receive too much of it and you quickly discover you are out of step not only with your own followers, but also with the rest of the world.

Leaders who want to follow make themselves accessible. They are highly visible to the company's workers and are available to talk with employees about making the company more successful.

Like Dan Schweiker of China Mist Tea, who is listed in research consultant Dale Dauten's book *The Gifted Boss*, successful managers know how to motivate and trust their employees. Schweiker, Dauten writes, was aware of the company's stuffy atmosphere. He changed it by replacing the conference table with a pool table.

> # Leading and following are opposite sides of the same coin.

3

Humility

W hen political cartoonist Mike Peters of the Dayton (Ohio) Daily News won the Pulitzer Prize for editorial cartooning in 1981, he was shocked. Like many prize winners, he never even considered himself in the running for such a prize, much less winning it.

Often it's the Mike Peterses of the world who get the most recognition. They're so busy working, they don't have time to follow their egos. Focusing on ourselves detracts from effective leadership. To be a leader requires humility.

Humility has many meanings: modesty, submission, meekness. Some of these don't correlate with the image that we have of powerful, capitalistic countries. In fact, the behaviors of many capitalist nations often are interpreted as lacking humility. We Americans, for example, are criticized for imposing our life-style—whether it is our government policies, popular culture, or technological advances—on other countries and cultures.

On corporate performance review forms, there's no category for humility. Usually we learn about it on our own. And frequently we learn it the hard way: That promotion doesn't come through. That person doesn't fall in love with us. The business we start goes belly-up. As a result we start to see ourselves as not quite the great person we thought we were.

The Big Picture

According to the Kabbalah, the text of Jewish mysticism, humility means understanding that everything we are depends on the Lord. If we are a great leader, that means we are a channel for the Lord to accomplish his work.

Joan of Arc, the patron saint of France, claimed that heavenly voices directed her on a divine mission to oppose the English invasion of France. She became a captain in the French army and a resistance leader in the Hundred Years War.

Seeing ourselves as dependent on someone or something other than ourselves is not a popular notion in America. Many of us have been trained to "stand on our own two feet" and make things happen. Humility gives us the option of no longer being entirely on our own.

Humility can also mean accepting our place in the universe. Some eighteenth-century philosophers referred to this idea as the Great Chain of Being, in which all creatures have their slot. Angels are higher than humans. Humans are higher than animals. This is also sometimes called hierarchy. Those who serve in the military learn humility quickly by accepting their rank and enduring a certain daily existence determined by that rank.

This aspect of humility has its critics in the modern world who contend, among other things, that accepting one's place may not always lead to progress. If Supreme Court Justice Thurgood Marshall had accepted his "place" as a black man "at the back of the bus," he never would have broken the color barrier for others in our schools and for himself.

Many business leaders, however, have learned to work with humility as they climbed the ladder of success.

- Henry Ford grew up on a farm near Greenfield, Michigan. When he incorporated the Ford Motor Co. in 1903, his efficient production-line methods allowed him to cut the cost of his product and increase wages. His workers' wages were the highest in the industry. He never forgot his humble beginnings and helped his workers enjoy a standard of living they might never have known otherwise.

- Stan Gault, CEO of Rubbermaid, is one of the most successful business leaders of our time. Time and again, he has come through for the shareholders pioneering new techniques and innovations for this company. But Gault doesn't advertise his success. He has never sought recognition; in fact, editors of business publications have sought him out as a role model for their readers. Management analysts have ventured to Rubbermaid's headquarters to learn his secrets, and competitors simply sit in awe as this giant of an executive delivers for all who are around him.

- Amazon.com Inc. chair and CEO Jeff Bezos developed a unique method for employing a talented staff. He directed his managers to hire skilled and gifted interviewees even if they were more skilled and talented than the managers themselves. Bezos taught his managers humility. They had to rise above any feelings of superiority or of being threatened by those more skilled than they. "If they don't hire them," Bezos said, "they'll be working for them down the road." By recognizing that only a winning staff could produce a winning product, Bezos raised the standards of his workforce.

The challenge is to accept the realities of one's existence but still hold out hope for a better life. The great leaders of the downtrodden always have worked to improve the condition of mankind.

Knowing Who We Are

Humility also means accurately assessing our value or worth. This involves self-knowledge and self-confidence. We neither overestimate nor underestimate our abilities.

- Founding father Thomas Jefferson knew his talent didn't lie in public speaking. Instead, he focused on writing, and bequeathed some of the most important written documents in the history of Western civilization, including the Declaration of Independence.

- Of all modern U.S. presidents, former President Gerald Ford probably had the most humble or accurate opinion of himself. Assuming office after Richard Nixon's resignation in the wake of Watergate, he refused to let the grandeur of the position affect his humble self-image. Because of his political roots in Congress and his status as an unelected president, Ford made a conscious effort to reverse the trappings of what historian Arthur Schlesinger termed the "imperial presidency," in which presidents grabbed more and more power for themselves within the federal government. He quietly met the challenges of an expanding inflation, a contracting economy, and chronic energy shortages.

- John J. "Joe" Ricketts, co-CEO of Ameritrade and a self-made billionaire, has led a modest life in Omaha, Nebraska. He has donated money to Boys Town and has assessed his worth and that of others in ways other than financial gain. As head of one of the leading companies in the financial services industry, Ricketts has regularly passed out kudos to his managers and employees. He has been one of the smartest members of the high-tech generation, but you would never know it if you sat next to him. He has taken no personal pride in his extraordinary knowledge and abilities and has gone out of his way to compliment all around him.

- Television talk-show host Oprah Winfrey has discussed her battles with weight control and her abusive childhood in front of her viewers. "I don't care if you have ten dollars or ten million dollars," she has said, "a fat butt is a fat butt." Winfrey's ability to acknowledge the obstacles she has encountered has enabled her to bond with millions of people. Despite her multi-million-dollar worth, her lavish lifestyle, and her superstar status, she has remained true to her Mississippi roots, which taught her to think positively and remain humble. "I've learned that if you focus on what you have, you'll end up having more. If you focus on what you lack, you will never have enough," she has said.

> ## The challenge is to know who we are but still be able to set a higher standard for who we want to be.

Sharing the Glory

Humility also means sharing the glory. Humble leaders realize they can't succeed without their followers. That's one reason corporations like Microsoft give their employees stock options. During the Chrysler turnaround, head of manufacturing Dick Dauch credited his team with everything from improvement in quality to quicker turnover of inventory.

- For many years, Quaker Oats has given a "teamwork" award. The award has been presented at the company's annual meeting and has reflected on workers from around the world who, together, have contributed to make something good happen for the company.

- Jacques Nasser, CEO of Ford Motor Co., instituted the Internet communication forum "Let's Chat," providing information about the state of the company and inviting regular correspondence and dialogue with employees. He has regularly shared compliments with those who have done well.

- Jerre L. Stead, chair of computer distributor Ingram Micro, has claimed he plans to share the money he received from stock options. In addition to family members, he has announced intentions to support Alzheimer's disease research, Northwestern University's Center for Ethics and Values, and religious and community organizations. The man whose business card referred to him as "coach" instead of "CEO" has valued the contributions of others.

Rewarding those who have helped us is a sign of humility.

Listening Instead of Talking

Humility also means being willing to listen. Whenever management consultant and leadership guru Stephen R. Covey (*The 7 Habits of Highly Effective People*) has coached new CEOs, he has told them to listen—if they want to learn what their company is all about.

- Marilyn Carlson Nelson, head of Carlson Companies, a leader in travel and leisure activities, has been known for her emphasis on drawing a circle and including everyone in it. She has reflected on this in the face of royalty and leading CEOs from around the world, demonstrating how important it is to be inclusive.

- Steven A. Raymund, CEO of Tech Data Corp. in Clearwater, Florida, has set up an electronic suggestion box, "Ask Steve," that allows the computer distributor's nine thousand employees worldwide to communicate with him directly. Workers are encouraged to e-mail him about such company policies as stock options, retirement plans, and personnel issues.

- More and more companies are holding meetings, conferences, seminars, and retreats for their employees. They are finding such events effective ways both to encourage communication between employee and management and to explain the company's mission to managers and their staff.

> ## Listening entails getting out of one's own head and opening up to what's going on in the world.

Moses, the Humble Leader

In learning to become more humble, we can gain insights from Moses. Although this great Hebrew commoner may appear anything but humble, consider how he got his start in life. The son of slaves, he should have died at birth, for the Pharaoh of Egypt had decreed that all Jewish male babies be killed. In hope of saving her child, Moses' mother put him in a waterproof container and set him afloat on the river—not a very promising beginning.

The Pharaoh's daughter found Moses and reared him as her own. But Moses felt alienated in Egypt: "I have been a stranger in a strange land" (Exod. 2:22). Like many immigrants who come to the United States, he was humbled by not having a sense of home.

Mission Impossible

In the beginning, Moses didn't see himself as a leader of the Israelites at all. He had spent most of his life as an Egyptian. Up to the time he heard the Lord at the Burning Bush, he hadn't shown himself as extraordinary in any way. In fact, Moses is described as "very meek" (Num. 12:3) when standing before his God.

When the Lord informed Moses that it was his mission to lead the children of Israel from Egypt to the Promised Land, Moses replied, "Who am I, that I should go unto Pharaoh" (Exod. 3:11). Moses gave myriad excuses to the Lord why he wasn't the one to lead the Israelites: that the people wouldn't believe he had been appointed by the Lord, and that he had a speech impediment: "I am slow of speech, and of a slow tongue" (Exod. 4:10).

As Moses pleaded his unworthiness, the Lord became angry. Moses lacked trust in something bigger than himself. When he finally realized that the Lord was serious, Moses humbly took on the mantle of leadership. He also immediately accepted help. The Lord told Moses that his brother, Aaron, could be his spokesperson.

To become humble, Moses surrendered himself to the Lord and believed he would get the resources he needed to accomplish his mission. After crossing the Red Sea, Moses led his people into the wilderness, where water and food were scarce. Desperate, Moses implored the Lord for help. Answering his prayer, the Lord sent quails for the Hebrews to net and rained down a white, breadlike substance. Moses' people were able to sustain themselves.

In our own world, it takes humility for students to turn themselves over to an institution of learning and be willing to be molded, or for athletes to submit to their coaches' rules to learn discipline and achieve athletic success.

Dependence

As Moses grew as a leader, he depended more and more on the Lord. Often Moses didn't understand the Lord's motives and knew he needed guidance. He recognized that he didn't have all the answers.

When, in humility, Moses cried out to the Lord that the burden of leadership was more than he could handle, he told the Lord, "I am not able to bear all this people alone, because it is too heavy for me" (Num. 11:14).

How many of our leaders have admitted to the heaviness of their burden and asked the help of a higher power?

Knowing His Identity

Like all humble leaders, Moses knew who he was and accepted his position as both leader of his people and servant of his Lord. Although the Lord said, "See, I have made thee a god to Pharaoh" (Exod. 7:1), Moses never acted like a deity. When the people stood up for Moses, Moses knew who was really being honored. "And it came to pass, when Moses went out unto the tabernacle, that all the people rose up, and stood every man at his tent door, and looked after Moses, until he was gone into the tabernacle" (Exod. 33:8).

Moses was able to differentiate who he was as a human being from the function he served in society. If our presidents and CEOs also understood the role they serve—a role that is separate from who they are—our institutions might work better, and retiring presidents and CEOs might not have such a hard time adjusting to life after they leave their jobs of influence.

Loyalty

In return for his loyalty to the Lord, the Lord was loyal to Moses. When Moses' brother, Aaron, and his sister, Miriam, became angry at Moses for marrying an Ethiopian woman, they questioned whether Moses was the Lord's only spokesperson. Maybe, they wondered, the Lord also was speaking through them. Maybe *they* should assume a more prominent role in leading the Israelites through the desert. But the Lord stood up for Moses. Appearing in the middle of a cloud at the door of the tabernacle, the Lord declared that Moses was his only spokesperson. He punished Miriam for her social bias and her defiance.

Loyalty requires tremendous humility. We have to embrace someone else's mission and goals. This means we have to sacrifice our ideas about what we think is right.

Not a "Yes Man"

But that doesn't mean Moses was a "yes man." When the Lord wanted to kill the rebellious children of Israel for plotting to murder Moses and Aaron and return to Egypt, Moses explained to the Lord why this would not be a wise course of action. Other nations, he reasoned, would interpret the Lord's anger as a failure to bring the Israelite people to the Promised Land. The Lord would not be seen as a powerful player in the Israelites' future. The Lord listened to Moses and relented.

Loyalty often means having the courage to speak up. Those in an organization who are humble, as opposed to those who seek to fulfill only their own goals, will take the risk to do whatever they consider necessary.

Not Taking All the Credit

Moses didn't take credit for his accomplishments. He told his people, "Hereby ye shall know that the Lord hath sent me to do all these works; for I have not done them of mine own mind" (Num. 16:28). Likewise, successful members of Alcoholics Anonymous, an organization that emphasizes humility, attribute their sobriety to a higher power, not to themselves.

> **Wise leaders acknowledge to whom the credit for their success is owed.**

The Benefits of Humility

A great deal can be gained by becoming more humble. Humility releases us from the bondage of self, allowing us to accomplish more. Leaders can't be self-absorbed. They have to be focused on their followers.

Humility also helps us to define who we are. Once we have a clear idea of our identity, we don't have to waste time analyzing ourselves.

In addition, humility enables us to share success and not take full responsibility for failure. Humble CEOs like Peter Larson understand their contributions and those of others. As head of Brunswick, Larson has been one of the movers and shakers in American business. He has received awards from the president, recognition from colleges and universities, and accolades from his business peers. He could easily live in an ivory tower. Instead, he's been out meeting his employees and greeting his customers, understanding their needs and always listening. If he's heard a good idea, he's been the first to implement it, never taking credit for what has been sent his way, but instead passing the real payoff along to the shareholders and the employees.

Today many Americans are struggling to balance humility with the country's four decades of narcissism. Author Tom Wolfe coined the 1960s as the "Me Decade"—and it's been "me, me, me" ever since. Recently, however, we seem to be tiring of our self-absorption. We're reaching out to find more meaning in our lives. Whether we're embracing religious or spiritual values—as demonstrated by the 15 percent increase in church attendance recorded by Protestant religions alone in 1998—or helping Kosovar refugees combat the ethnic cleansing in Yugoslavia, or recognizing the rights of animals in scientific research, as a nation we're beginning to look outside ourselves and assume greater responsibility in the world.

Those Who Have Been Humble

There are many examples of humility among people of note.

- Princess Diana devoted much of her time to sick children, land-mine victims, and AIDS patients. Being a privileged member of English society didn't stop her from traveling around the world to show her empathy with those who were ravaged by war and disease. As the "people's princess," Diana's high profile and popularity brought criticism from England's royal family but endeared her to the public. Unlike Sarah Ferguson, Duchess of York, whose search for worldwide publicity through her ventures into children's book publishing and weight-loss programs brought her ridicule, Diana's ability to reach out beyond the elitism of the monarchy made her a leading representative of her country.

- John Coleman, former president of Haverford College, has always had a thirst for learning. While he was president of Haverford, Coleman temporarily left the college to try his hand at different occupations, including garbage collector and prison guard. He has been a rare breed of educator, never seeking attention or personal gain, like many of his colleagues have. After retiring from Haverford—and determined to keep growing—he ran an inn and accepted a job editing a newspaper.

- General Colin Powell, former chairman of the Joint Chiefs of Staff, grew up in a poor neighborhood in Brooklyn and rose to become a four-star general. He has always maintained close ties to the black community. Today he is a leading spokesperson for educational opportunities for disadvantaged youth.

- Despite her upper-class upbringing, Eleanor Roosevelt became a champion for the poor and downtrodden. As the wife of President Franklin Delano Roosevelt, she often influenced the president's social welfare policies, and was more popular with many Americans than he. A shy child born to a legendary beauty, she overcame a lifelong battle with what some called her homely looks to become a successful public spokesperson, many times on behalf of her husband. Unlike some of the first ladies who followed her into the White House, she was never given to excess while offering little in return.

- A schoolteacher from Milwaukee, Wisconsin, Golda Meir became one of Israel's greatest prime ministers. Although a mother figure to the nation, her steely determination led her country to victory during the Yom Kippur War in the early 1970s. Unlike one of her successors, Benjamin Netanyahu, who was forced out of office, she maintained close ties to her followers while leading them through difficult times.

- Lou Gehrig was the "pride of the Yankees," the iron horse who, in his day, had played more consecutive games than any player in baseball history. Upon retiring from baseball due to a crippling disease, Gehrig told sixty thousand fans that he was the luckiest man on the face of the earth to be so recognized.

Those Who Were Too Proud

The proud or narcissistic include the following.

- Walt Disney so loved his work with Mickey Mouse and other creations that he forgot to acknowledge the needs and desires of his subordinates at Walt Disney Company. When his employees asked him for more money, he ignored them. He assumed they were lucky enough just to be working for his company. Disney didn't realize that the company would shut down without their input. When the staff went on strike, he was deeply hurt. His lack of humility prevented him from taking care of the men and women who helped make his company successful.

- When he was president of the United States, Richard Nixon thought he was above the law. He believed he could rely on the doctrine of executive privilege to protect him from having to obey the country's criminal laws that were broken during the cover-up of the Watergate break-in. Nixon's lack of humility ended his presidency. Once the Supreme Court decided that the doctrine of executive privilege did not allow him to withhold evidence of his involvement in the cover-up, he resigned under threat of impeachment and removal.

- As head of Creative Artists Agency, Michael Ovitz enjoyed a reputation as one of the most powerful men in Hollywood. Thirsting to be an even more powerful player in the entertainment industry, he left CAA to become president of Walt Disney Company. Ovitz assumed that his job at Disney would allow him to control a media empire. After only fourteen months, his assumption proved false and he lost his job.

- Janet Cooke, a *Washington Post* reporter in the early 1980s, wrote a story about an eight-year-old heroin addict named Jimmy. After winning a Pulitzer Prize for that story, questions were raised about its validity. Ultimately, Cooke admitted that Jimmy in fact did not exist and that she had fabricated the story. She resigned from her position in disgrace. Cooke's lack of humility kept her from pursuing the truth and led to one of journalism's major scandals.

How to Become Humble

How can we become humble? It's not easy in America. But there are plenty of role models of effective leaders and their use of humility. They share many characteristics.

✓ **Practice Prayer**

Humble leaders pray to someone or something. Books such as Philip Dunn's *Prayer: Language of the Soul* are helping us learn to pray on a regular basis, as part of our daily routine. Prayer actually is a very simple process. Billions of people throughout the centuries have had no trouble praying. Prayer means turning our attention from our own being to another being. It lifts us from ourselves. In Alcoholics Anonymous, atheists coming into the program are counseled to designate anyone or anything but themselves—from a squirrel to the ocean—as their higher power.

Prayer can be as short a request as "Help me to stop worrying about my work" or "Give me guidance about where I should send my son to college." Prayer is miraculous. Help does come. Leaders who don't pray are doing a disservice to their followers.

✓ **Accept Ourselves**

Being comfortable in our own skin can become an important component of humility. Robert Kennedy recognized that he was different from his father and his brothers Joe and Jack, whom he admired. He did the best with the qualities he had. And he succeeded. His vision of equal rights for all Americans made him a popular candidate for the Democratic presidential nomination in 1968.

Many self-help programs encourage their members who are searching for inner peace to write an inventory of their strengths and weaknesses. This inventory is then shared with someone the individual trusts. Frequently, people come away from this experience less concerned about themselves.

Some executives go on a retreat to a monastery to reflect on who they are and who they can be. Even talking with an old friend can be useful in getting us to accept ourselves.

✔ Use Humor

Humble leaders know how to laugh. Humor is comic distancing. Laughter lets us move far enough away from a subject to have perspective. During the worst of the Chrysler financial crisis, workers never knew if the company would open its doors the next morning. They handled the big unknowns by making jokes. After his assassination attempt, former President Ronald Reagan cracked a few jokes from his hospital bed. That took some of the focus off his condition and relaxed those who were worried about him and the leadership of the nation.

✔ Learn to Trust

Humble leaders can trust. They can delegate tasks to others and expect that the jobs will get done. The most effective leaders find the right people to do what has to get done. As a result, they're relaxed and accessible.

Since the 1960s we have lost trust in many of our institutions, from our schools to our corporations. If we want to regain trust, we can start by taking baby steps. We can slowly come to trust our child's teacher or a colleague at work. As we're doing that, we'll find out what aspects of them are less than trustworthy and work around those. Total distrust leaves us isolated.

> ## Trust is our link to the world
> ## outside ourselves.

✓ **Find Heroes**

Humble leaders seek out heroes. If we reach out to people we admire, we raise the bar on our own performance. Hillary Clinton greatly admired former first lady Eleanor Roosevelt and looked to her example to provide a role model for leadership. When he was thinking about becoming a political figure, Yale law student Bill Clinton looked to the example of John F. Kennedy and Connecticut legislator Joe Lieberman.

Heroes help us look beyond ourselves. They don't need to be famous people. The two Polish immigrants who help my family and take care of our house are heroes to me. They have problems, everything from not knowing the language to trying to bring their relatives to America from Poland. Yet they take life as it is. They don't complain. They don't seem to resent the process of building a better life for themselves and their family.

The Future of Humility

Humility may have a good future in America. The world has become so complex that many of us have realized no one person has all the answers. We expect our medical doctor to help us stay well but not to give us advice on real estate or investments. We expect our boss to guide the team but not to try to play Dr. Freud. We expect Kraft Foods to provide us with cheese and gelatin but not computer expertise.

Those who assume that they can be all things to all people or all occasions are now considered arrogant. Being humble is the way to dignity in an uncertain universe.

Humility helps us find our finest selves.

4

Self-control

Five years ago a successful executive went for his annual physical. He was jubilant because his company had just gotten an account it had been after for a number of years. The doctor asked this man how long he wanted to live. The man answered that he had to live long enough to see his two young sons launched in the world. The doctor said, "Forget that. You have about six months to live."

The man was suffering from the effects of obesity. His heart was working too hard to support his 400 pounds of weight. He had two options: lose weight or die. The man decided to lose weight. Today he is still with us. He weighs under 200 pounds. And when he started eating differently, he also started thinking differently. He became more successful than ever. Self-control saved his life and helped his career.

Self-control is important. With it we can lose weight, train for a marathon, obey the law, avoid obstacles in the road to success. Without it, we surrender to the worst of our human traits: self-indulgence, anger, recklessness, selfishness, self-righteousness.

The Marshmallow Test

Self-control pays high dividends. This was demonstrated through the Marshmallow Test, the famous study on delaying gratification that was conducted in the 1960s at Stanford University. Psychologist Walter Mischel gave each of his four-year-old subjects a marshmallow and told them that if they could delay eating it until he came back from running an errand, he would give them two marshmallows. The children were later tracked through high school; those who were able to exert self-control and delay gratification exhibited more social competence, self-reliance, confidence, and increased scores on college entrance exams. As adolescents they were more dependable, more assertive, and better able to cope with the frustrations of life than those who, years earlier, could not wait for two marshmallows.

Self-Control and Leadership

Self-control is the foundation of trust. If our country is threatened by an aggressive enemy, we count on our leaders to weigh all the options and implement the appropriate strategic action. If our company is losing revenue, we count on our CEO to choose the right plan to bring back profits. We depend on our leaders to be in control.

A leader without self-control can be unpredictable and dangerous. Some of the worst crimes against humanity in modern history have been perpetrated by those who lacked self-control.

- Adolf Hitler single-handedly defines a leader who was out of control. The fascist dictator's contempt for humanity allowed him to massacre millions of people whom he had labeled as undeserving of life. Among his targets were Jews, Communists, homosexuals, and gypsies. Unable to control his desire to rule the world, he manipulated an entire country for his own purpose. "What good fortune for those in power that people do not think," he said. To this day Hitler is remembered as a dangerous leader and a man without a soul.

- A rival of Hitler in his lack of concern for human life, Joseph Stalin purportedly murdered as many as twelve million Russians in his push to reform the Soviet Union. He moved the U.S.S.R. from a preindustrial nation to a major player on the world stage over the graves of starved and murdered workers. "A single death is a tragedy; a million deaths is a statistic," he said. Stalin's legacy was one of forced-labor camps and a society of secret police whose tactics were marked by brutality.

- Iraqi dictator and president Saddam Hussein has purged and murdered dozens of government officials, religious leaders, and even family members who challenged his authority. He has used chemical weapons to crush the Kurdish sect in northern Iraq and courted international disfavor by refusing to comply with the terms of the treaty that ended the Gulf War. Of

Hussein, former President George Bush remarked, "We're dealing with Hitler revisited." Unrepentant, Hussein has exerted no self-control over any actions that further his cause, no matter how inhumane they may be.

- In the 1980s and 1990s, Yugoslavian President Slobodan Milosevic championed ethnic cleansing in Bosnia and Kosovo, killing and forcing hundreds of thousands of people from their homes in a blatant act of ethnic hatred. In 1999, during the NATO air strike against the Serbian military, he was indicted by the International Criminal Tribunal for the Former Yugoslavia on charges of murder, mass deportation, and other crimes against humanity.

The Greek word for self-control is *egkrateia*, meaning "holding oneself in." I once knew an executive who was a real screamer. Everyone lived in fear of him. He often lost his temper during meetings, throwing china around and kicking over chairs. Even when he was absent from the meetings that took place in the room on the other side of his office, he would turn up the volume on a tape he had made of himself yelling and screaming, reminding everyone that he was a force to be reckoned with. This always added an air of sobriety—and fear—to the meetings.

Wise leaders don't rush into action.

- During the Gulf War, Israeli leaders exercised self-control after the country was bombed by Iraqi scud missiles. Rather than return fire and risk both an escalation in the war and further enmity from some of its already hostile Arab neighbors, Israel used restraint and left the fighting of the war to the allied coalition.

- Retail industry giant Wal-Mart delayed bolstering its online retail efforts despite the explosion of electronic commerce on the Web by its competitors. By not rushing into this new field, Wal-Mart has followed what may be a policy of restraint while developing its new operation.

- Businessman Richard C. Hyde, a personal friend of mine, has extraordinary self-control. In situation after situation, I have seen him hold his temper and hold back on his opinion to clients until it was absolutely necessary for him to come forward and offer it. Time and again, his self-control has paid off. He has achieved outstanding results with his clients.

What Leaders Do

Haven't we always experienced our leaders as people of action? Our greatest political, historical, and religious leaders tend to be defined by their achievements, not their restraint.

- In the fifteenth century, Christopher Columbus aggressively sought funding to establish a new trade route to India and prove that the world was round.

- During the Revolutionary War, George Washington led twenty-four hundred men across the icy Delaware River to surprise the English troops. The ensuing battle marked a turning point in the war for the morale of the American patriots.

- After his election to the presidency in 1933, Franklin Delano Roosevelt put into effect the social and economic reforms that comprised the New Deal and pulled the country out of the Great Depression.

- In January 1998 the seventy-seven-year-old religious leader and anti-Communist crusader Pope John Paul II traveled to Cuba and met with Socialist dictator Fidel Castro. His open-air masses helped revitalize religious commitment in a country whose population increasingly began to seek peace and understanding from its leaders.

What Leaders Don't Do

Often, what leaders don't do is as important as what they do.

- Mahatma Gandhi saw as his mission the freedom of his country from its English colonizers. He led his people by practicing nonviolent resistance. Controlling their temptation to resort to violence, the people of India won their freedom without firing a shot.

- Senator John McCain of Arizona was a naval aviator during the Vietnam War. In 1967 he was shot down, captured, and imprisoned. When he was offered an early release as part of a propaganda ploy by the Vietnamese military, McCain refused. His sense of honor and patriotism came at a huge price: he was tortured and imprisoned (and held in solitary confinement) for five and a half years.

- When Jackie Robinson became the nation's first African American to play on a major-league team in more than half a century, he learned a fast lesson in self-control. He knew he would have to battle prejudice from opposing players in the league. Accepting owner Branch Rickey's offer to join the Brooklyn Dodgers, Robinson promised, "There will be no incident." Throughout his first season in the majors, however, pitchers hurled fastballs dangerously close to his head and runners slid with the spikes of their shoes aimed at his legs. Off the field, in Southern towns that practiced segregation, Robinson was equally humiliated. Through it all, he didn't falter. He kept his self-control and his promise. By resisting the temptation to fight back, he gained the respect of his fans and fellow players, was voted Rookie of the Year, and helped win the pennant for the Dodgers. He became the first black man elected to baseball's Hall of Fame.

- Natan Scharansky was a famous Russian "refusenik" and a thorn in the Soviet Union's side during the 1970s and 1980s. A defender of political and religious freedom, he was imprisoned by the KGB, often under solitary confinement, while his wife gained her freedom and relocated to Israel. Always fighting the KGB's attempts to break his spirit, Scharansky managed to adhere to the dietary laws of his religion and to maintain his faith. He didn't cave in to the KGB's attempts to weaken him. Eventually, his case won international recognition and he was released by the Soviets. Scharansky exercised self-control up until the end of his imprisonment. A hero of Russia's political and religious prisoners, he settled in Israel with his wife and became a government leader.

Self-control makes or breaks leaders. It did with Moses.

Losing Control

Moses was an imperfect man. Some of his mistakes were due to loss of self-control.

Years of Exile
When he was a prince of Egypt, Moses saw an Egyptian guard beating a Hebrew slave. He rushed forward to save the man and, without thinking, killed the Egyptian. The consequence of Moses' loss of control was a life in exile. He had to flee the only life he knew.

Running the Whole Show
When he became leader of his people, Moses took sole responsibility for the entire community. He taught the people about the Lord and his laws. He answered all their questions. He acted as judge in disputes between neighbors. From morning until night, he was surrounded by the people whose needs he was to serve. Before long, he had lost perspective on how much responsibility he could handle. He lost control of his ability to set limits.

Losing His Temper
When, as leader of the Israelites, Moses returned from Mount Sinai with the Ten Commandments, he saw hundreds of his people worshiping a golden calf, dancing naked and having sex before it. Seeing their ecstasy before a false idol infuriated him. Moses succumbed to his rage and lost control. He smashed the tablets into pieces and ordered those followers who did not participate in the idolatrous act to kill those who did. Instead of executing only the ringleaders, his

loss of control brought terror and chaos to the entire community.

Giving His All to His Mission

While Moses' dedication to his mission was never questioned, his loyalties to his wife and two sons were. His attention to the Lord and the nation of Israel made his family feel like second-class citizens. Like many workaholics today who lose track of their priorities, the job came first.

Facing the Consequences

These losses of control on Moses' part had consequences even he could not foresee.

Fleeing into the wilderness after killing the Egyptian, Moses became an outcast. Whereas he was once part of a community, now he couldn't even join his parents and siblings and his people, the Hebrew slaves, with whom he belonged.

While leading the Israelites through the wilderness and tirelessly continuing to resolve their squabbles, Moses didn't realize he was overworking himself until his father-in-law, Jethro, forcefully called it to his attention. "Thou will surely wear away, both thee and this people that is with thee: for this thing is too heavy for thee" (Exod. 18:18). Ruling on disputes was taking too long. As the people waited to have their day in court, their resentments against their neighbors festered. By not being in control of himself, Moses began to lose control of his people.

When Moses flew into a rage upon seeing his people worshiping the golden calf, his lapse in leadership had dire consequences. He betrayed his people, for they suffered the deaths of their friends and family and saw their leader out of control.

Moses' inability to devote himself to his family resulted in a personal tragedy. Unable to compete with the Lord or the Israelites, his wife, Zipporah, left the Israelites' camp and returned to her father, Jethro. Moses was excessive in his attentions to his followers, but lacking in his responsibilities at home.

Throughout history when a leader is censured, his followers often also suffer. During World War II, Japan's military leaders exhibited an excessive and aggressive expansionist policy toward China and Southeast Asia and brought the United States into the war. When the atomic bomb was dropped on Nagasaki and Hiroshima, the Japanese people suffered enormous physical and psychological hardships.

**A leader without self-control
is unpredictable and dangerous.**

Blind Anger

It's easy to lose control. You get angry with a co-worker. Your child disobeys you. You lose your job. You don't think about the consequences of your actions at first.

Moses usually could be depended on for exercising great control when dealing with the complaining Israelites. He understood how hard it was for them to leave a predictable, although demoralizing, life in Egypt for an uncertain one in the wilderness. Often he interceded before an angry God on behalf of his people when they expressed doubt or lack of faith.

However, when Moses saw the golden calf, his anger erupted. He didn't stop to consider why the people might have disobeyed him. He didn't think about his part in their rebellion.

Had he been gone too long? Were the people afraid without their leader? Should he have sent a sign that he was returning soon?

Staying Connected

While Moses was on Mount Sinai receiving the Ten Commandments, he was not in touch with his people. On the mountain he operated on a high spiritual plane. It was easy to forget the fragility of human nature.

Moses strayed too far spiritually and physically from his people. Like him, many have lost perspective on their mission of leadership.

- Benjamin Netanyahu won the position of prime minister of Israel with a platform that advocated greater security for Israel and a tougher stance on negotiations with the Arabs. When the mood of the country shifted to a more conciliatory one and the people expressed a greater desire for peace, Netanyahu maintained his confrontational style and demonstrated an inability to make concessions. Having lost touch with the people's wishes, Netanyahu resoundingly lost his title as prime minister and resigned as the head of his party.

- England's Queen Elizabeth II kept herself at the traditional royal distance from her subjects. However, as the British people became more tolerant of public displays of emotion and sought less emotional restraint from their queen, Elizabeth's aloofness and stoicism led to accusations that she was disconnected from the people. Observers began to wonder if the time had come to redefine the role of the monarchy.

Leaders can't roam too far from their followers.

Leader Knows Best?

Moses was in the unique position of being able to communicate directly with God. This set him apart from the Israelites. Like many leaders, though, Moses' status may have caused him to feel that he was the most important link in the chain. He saw himself as indispensable. He believed that only he could get things done correctly. Sitting in judgment over his followers, Moses believed that he had the right to do what he did, and that the people were wrong.

In short, Moses suffered from self-righteousness. Although he was humble before God, he failed to lead his people with the empathy and patience they needed. It's easy for leaders to become convinced that they're the only ones who know the truth.

Regaining Control

After fleeing Egypt, Moses lived in the wilderness with a Midian tribe, learning a new trade and establishing a family. As a valued member of this community, he regained control over his life. Later, as leader of the Israelites, he listened to the words of his father-in-law, Jethro, and began to delegate some important functions, such as religious education and dispensing justice to others in the community. In this way he organized the wandering Hebrews just like the CEOs of corporations organize their companies. He established a clear chain of command—a must for all leaders. Moses' followers received more individual attention and a quicker resolution of their disputes. Fortunately, he saw the wisdom of Jethro's advice.

Another story of excessive zeal in work didn't have such a happy ending. An engineer by training, former President Jimmy Carter took an engineer's approach to leadership. Instead of acting like a chief executive who sets policies and allows others to enact them, Carter tried to micromanage the running of the country. He got bogged down in the more trivial details of management and subjected himself to criticism when he made the wrong decisions. He couldn't set the overall policy of his administration or change course when he made a mistake. He wasn't re-elected for a second term.

After his followers were punished for worshiping the golden calf, Moses returned to his job of guiding the Israelites through the wilderness. He saw that his people had no direction and invited those who were interested in following the Lord to join him. He restored order to the community. He also returned to Mount Sinai and, prostrating himself in prayer before the Lord, requested another set of tablets. In addition to the Ten Commandments, Moses received a "heavenly commentary" to help his people better understand the laws.

Many leaders have regained self-control, sometimes against great odds.

- Realizing they had lost control by becoming hopeless alcoholics, Bill Wilson and Dr. Bob Smith turned to each other for a way out of their addiction. Through their efforts they discovered a way to help millions of fellow alcoholics around the world. As co-founders of Alcoholics Anonymous, Bill W. and Dr. Bob initiated a twelve-step program for overcoming their disease that not only has been endorsed by medical experts, but also has become the guidepost for many other self-help programs.

- Best-selling author Dale Carnegie transformed a lack of control into a philosophy that has helped millions. At the start of his sales career, Carnegie was a failure. He could not manage his emotions. When he had to speak or meet new business contacts, he became paralyzed with fright. The more he attempted to conquer his fear, the more anxious he became. Carnegie decided to put himself back on track. His personal quest for confidence turned into a self-help empire with the success of his first book, *How to Win Friends and Influence People.* With more than 10 million copies in print, Carnegie's approach to public speaking and the art of selling has benefited countless individuals, making his name synonymous with success.

- When he starred as Superman in a series of films, actor Christopher Reeve portrayed a superhero who was always in control. In real life he lost the use of most of his body after severing his spine in a riding accident. Refusing to be imprisoned by his broken body, Reeve began an extensive physical therapy campaign that has allowed him to function in the world and maintain his career. Reeve gained back his life by controlling his determination. Without self-control, he would have lapsed into self-pity. Today he is an active spokesperson for the disabled.

We Are All Moses

Moses was a typical leader. It's difficult to think of any leader in history who has always been in full control of himself. Perhaps it's part of human nature to lose our balance. Like Moses, there are many who have lost control.

- The musical genius Wolfgang Amadeus Mozart was like a fine racehorse. His performance was exquisite, but like racehorses, he rode himself to exhaustion— and death. A prolific composer, at one point in his life he wrote three symphonies in seven months. Driven to write and perform since he was a child, he lacked the inner set of controls that tell us when to stop and rest. Succumbing to emotional despair and ill health, he met an untimely death at the age of thirty-five, leaving humankind to wonder how many more masterpieces he would have left as his legacy.

- Ross Johnson, the onetime CEO of RJR Nabisco, was notorious for his excesses. He believed in change so much that, on a whim, he moved the corporate headquarters of his multi-billion-dollar company from New York City to Atlanta. Unable to reward the achievements of others, he repeatedly juggled executive positions, ordering a vice president to change positions with the person who reported to him or her. Due to his impulsive actions and business decisions, he eventually lost control of the company, as well as his job.

- The presidency of William Jefferson Clinton will forever be remembered for his excesses. Alongside any legacy of economic and international leadership, the president's time in the White House will be shadowed by scandal and the repeated mistrust of his followers. Bill Clinton lost his balance. Like England's King Henry VIII, he allowed his appetites to get out of control.

- Al Dunlap, known in corporate America as "Chainsaw Al" for his penchant for slashing jobs to improve corporate performance, turned Scott Paper Company into a Wall Street success story and was recruited to save the stumbling Sunbeam corporation. His first move at Sunbeam was to fire nearly half of the company's twelve thousand employees. Convinced of his invincibility, this "Rambo in pinstripes" indulged himself by acquiring other companies, including Coleman Co., Signature USA Inc., and First Alert Inc., increasing Sunbeam's debt by $2.5 billion in the process. To pay for his purchases, he cut an additional sixty-four hundred jobs from his empire. As the company spiraled out of control, the board of directors lost confidence in Dunlap. After he was fired, he appeared on a business television show in tears, unable to understand what had happened to him.

- The work of legendary filmmaker and brilliant satirist Woody Allen, who commands free rein in his movies, is characterized by self-indulgence. His once-wide audience has diminished to die-hard fans because of his ongoing emotional anguish, fear of death, and attraction to neurotic relationships. His excessive behavior on-screen has found expression in his off-screen life.

Many leaders, however, have sought change through self-control.

- The former comedian, actor, and author Dick Gregory had an epiphany when he confronted the shocking lack of human rights in our country. Realizing that being excessively overweight prevented him from becoming an effective spokesperson, he shed pounds and gained the physical energy necessary to devote himself to human and civil rights causes. His commitment to boost his own self-control and image has made a lasting impact on society.

- Former first lady Betty Ford confronted her dependency on alcohol by checking herself into a clinic for alcoholism treatment. Her actions helped bring about national recognition of alcoholism addiction as a serious disease affecting thousands of Americans. She has inspired many others to work for the recognition of alcoholism as an illness that requires treatment.

Learning Self-control

From the success enjoyed by many authors of self-help books, it is clear that Americans want a better life. In order to meet our goals, however, we need self-control. How do we get it?

Self-control comes to different people at different times and through different avenues. Some people come to it because they can't afford not to. Maybe they're diagnosed with a serious disease. Maybe they've lost too many jobs and their careers are on the line. These people realize that their current way of seeing the world and behaving no longer works.

No matter why or how we become transformed, there are a number of strategies for achieving self-control. We can utilize them at many different times in our lives, for self-discipline is a life's work.

✓ **Learn Acceptance**

Accepting the universe, or at least those parts of it that we can't change, is an important component of self-control. Had Moses accepted the Children of Israel just as they were, he might not have lost control when he came down from Mount Sinai. He would have punished only the most guilty. By acknowledging that the people were stubborn, anxious, and ungrateful, he wouldn't have been so shocked by their behavior and would have labored to change it.

Acceptance is the basis of many self-help organizations, such as those that are modeled on the Twelve-Step program. Members of these groups recite the Serenity Prayer. The prayer is short and simple:

> *God, grant me the*
> *Serenity to accept the things*
> *I cannot change,*
> *Courage to change the things I can; and the*
> *Wisdom to know the difference.*

Acceptance can help all of us. This has become evident to me in numerous circumstances.

One of the toughest jobs in Manhattan is driving a cab. When a dignitary comes to visit the streets are blocked. Often a water main happens to break, adding to the congestion. There's a great deal of ongoing construction work. Traffic is jammed. The cab drivers I've spoken with who were earning the most money and had the greatest serenity said that they simply accept the traffic as it is. The others gave me a blow-by-blow account of their daily ordeals and had dreams of doing something else.

About a month ago our office lost a client. In trying to examine what had gone wrong, I asked myself what we could have changed in how we handled this type of account. Before accepting my staff's meaningful and breakthrough suggestions, I first had to accept the fact that we may have been doing things that were detrimental.

✔ Walk in Someone Else's Shoes

Until you walk in someone else's shoes, you have no idea what he or she really is going through. When we feel what others are feeling, we're less likely to react.

When Moses saw the golden calf, he might have asked himself: "What must the Chosen People be feeling to do something like this?"

Former President Ronald Reagan was a leader with a great capacity for empathy. His administration enjoyed many accomplishments. That's because the American people, knowing that they were being understood, were willing to cooperate with him.

In their provocative article "The Set-Up-to-Fail Syndrome: How Bosses Create Their Own Poor Performance" (*Harvard Business Review*), Jean-François Manzoni and Jean-Louis Basoux place the burden of learning why their followers act the way they do on the business leader. According to Manzoni and Basoux, it's the leader's responsibility to figure out and remedy the reasons behind subordinates' unsatisfactory performances. Their thesis is a welcome remedy to the unresolved personnel problems that exist in many American businesses.

> ## Leaders need to be trained to understand why their followers are acting the way they are.

✓ **Learn from Failure**

Failure, a not-so-gentle teacher, forces us to look at what we're doing. It's the universe telling us to get our house back in order.

In the late 1980s, Shell Oil Company responded to falling oil prices by downsizing and laying off employees. What began as an attempt to survive a changed economy evolved into a company dynamic with ominous portents: profits remained low and employee morale suffered. Shell's failure to respond more appropriately to the crisis led its executives toward a reengineering of the company and the search for a better solution.

In the early 1990s, IBM's stock slid from 178 to 49. The computer technology leader found itself slipping behind its rivals in nearly every one of its divisions. Its giant and lumbering corporate structure was unable to adapt quickly to a marketplace that, due to technological advances, was changing every six to nine months. CEO John Akers didn't take the firm's failure seriously enough. As the company continued to drift downward, employees who hadn't been fired began deserting ship. Because of his inability to take the signs of trouble seriously, Akers was forced out.

Those American businesses that experience failure in the global marketplace must get their excesses under control. If they don't recognize the warning signs, the companies simply will continue to descend in a downward spiral.

> **From failure often comes success.**

✔ **Follow Instructions**

When all else fails, follow instructions. Following a set game plan is a proven way to get control of ourselves. Even some of the rudest, crudest executives who attend Dale Carnegie's easy-to-follow seminars to learn social poise and grace succeed just by following the rules in class. This may not be rocket science, but the results can be amazing. Jobs can be saved, for example, when the company's executive simply deals more effectively with his or her subordinates.

It's not unusual to panic when we don't know what to do. Like Moses, we spin out and lose control. Perhaps the best way to get back on our feet is to study how others have approached the same situation and choose the best fit for us. When Moses saw the community of Israelites in disarray, perhaps the best thing he could have done was to march back up the mountain and ask the Lord for instructions on how to deal with the situation.

The Benefits of Self-control

A nation, a leader, an ordinary citizen—anyone who has self-control—can change the world. It doesn't take much to set events in motion.

Women's rights activist Gloria Steinem loves to tell audiences that the single flap of a butterfly's wing can change the weather pattern across the world. So, too, with personal behavior. A little less overspending. A little less anxiety. A little more kindness.

Even with small changes, leaders can have a tremendous effect on the world. Businesses can be run more effectively. Parents can raise happier children. Relationships can be more fulfilling. Those responsible for making decisions can admit that they don't have all the answers and can ask for help. Wars may not erupt so quickly.

Self-control
is the genetic code
for leadership.

5

Gratitude

> One night, as he was walking to his car after attending a black-tie dinner party, Birch Foracker, a powerful executive at Ma Bell when that company was the only telephone company around, came upon a manhole. Inside were several telephone company employees struggling to repair an emergency breakdown. Tuxedo and all, Foracker climbed down into the manhole and thanked each man for working so late. Somewhere along the line, he had learned to say those tough two words: thank you.

Whether you say it in German, Bulgarian, Korean, or Taiwanese, "thank you" expresses an important statement: "Hey, I couldn't have done it on my own. I know you've helped me, and I appreciate it."

Expressing gratitude is a form of admitting that we're interdependent. None of us can exist without a little help from friends, family, employees, government, and some higher being.

Gratitude is universal. One of the first things mothers teach young children is to say thank you. Being grateful is the first step in socialization. It helps us realize that we're not the center of the universe.

A Problem for Moses

The Chosen People never openly gave thanks. Instead of focusing on what they had, and being grateful for it, they frequently complained about what they didn't have or what they used to have. Most of the time in the desert they were miserable.

And most of the time, they made Moses miserable, too. He had his hands full with the daily chore of listening to griping, unappreciative, disenchanted, rebellious people who never seemed to have enough. They complained of thirst; they complained of hunger. When they were given water to drink and food to eat, they complained that there wasn't enough variety in their diet. They were so good at complaining, they even tested the Lord's patience: "How long will this people provoke me? And how long will it be ere they believe me, for all the signs which I have shewed among them?" (Num. 14:11).

Giving Thanks

We all know people who are ungrateful. Perhaps we ourselves have been guilty of it, too. Unable to see the whole picture, we didn't appreciate what we had. Perhaps our salaries were not as high as we would have liked, but our benefits package was exceptional. Perhaps we were not as thin as a supermodel, but we were in good health. Perhaps our teenagers were not "A" students, but they didn't smoke, drink, or take drugs.

Like Abbie Hoffman, co-founder of the 1960s Yippie anti-establishment movement, we weren't grateful for the good things around us. Hoffman told America's youth never to trust anyone over thirty. He hated the Establishment and spoke endlessly about what was wrong with the country.

Hoffman seemed unable to give thanks for some of the wonderful principles the United States stands for, or to find a place for himself in the country he had so maligned. He died alone and penniless in an apartment in Bucks County, Pennsylvania. He had taken 150 phenobarbital pills and washed them down with alcohol.

The Power of Gratitude

Lack of gratitude may not be life endangering, but it certainly isn't life enhancing. In a capitalistic society, it's easy to keep reaching for more—more money, more power, more success. We forget to step back and appreciate what we have. Our leaders can help. By their example, they remind us of the power of thanks.

- John Tu and David Sun, co-founders of Kingston Technology Co. in California, give annual bonuses to their one thousand employees. Since 1997, the company has awarded each employee from $20,000 to $69,000, based on tenure and performance, helping to foster a sense of family at the company. "We've had complaints from other companies that we're too generous," admitted one of the company's vice presidents. Tu and Sun are leaders in showing companies how to express their gratitude to hardworking and loyal employees.

- John Gutfreund, former CEO and chair of Salomon Brothers investment house, has been a leading Wall Street figure for more than three decades. He has given back to society in many ways, including contributing his time and expertise as director of numerous corporations and not-for-profit organizations. He is an example of someone who knows that the money he has accumulated (he is a millionaire many times over) is only relative to the happiness it can bring. Gutfreund has made expressing gratitude one of many personal achievements.

- When she was head of the American Red Cross, Elizabeth Dole regularly went out of her way to thank people all over the world for the efforts they made to help people in need. In the past she quietly visited inner-city facilities for the poor and sick with no notice to the media.

How many award-winning scientists, athletes, actors, politicians, journalists—leaders in their fields—upon accepting their awards, thank others for helping them in their achievements?

Gratitude can be transforming. When we become grateful, our attitude changes from a negative to a positive one.

- At a meeting of Al-Anon, a branch of Alcoholics Anonymous for family members whose relatives have drinking problems, a man talked about his lousy childhood. He complained that years of therapy had not worked to heal him. The group leader gave the man a choice: he could feel sorry for the rest of his life, or he could give thanks for being tough enough to survive and able to tell the tale.

- Many cancer patients cope with the effects of chemotherapy on their immune system, their hair, their muscles, and their general physical condition. Some of them rise above the temptation to give into self-pity and recognize what they have to be thankful for: the availability of treatment, friends, family, a job to go back to, or a promising survival rate. Their positive attitude is often a powerful tool for combating their illness.

The power of gratitude can transform organizations and nations as well as people. Giving back to the community is one way individuals, organizations, and governments express gratitude for the successes they enjoy.

- More than most companies in Los Angeles, the Atlantic Richfield Co. has contributed its executives' time and substantial funds to the city's civic culture. A leader in corporate citizenship, the company organized a "Save The Books" program after a fire nearly destroyed the city's Central Library; helped small businesses recover from the 1992 riots that devastated the city after the verdict in the criminal trial of the four police officers accused of beating motorist Rodney King; contributed to buildings for the homeless and the arts; and initiated many other works that engaged the company in the community. "One of the traditions of leadership," says Russell Sakaguchi, executive director of the Arco Foundation, "is to realize it's a much bigger thing than your involvement."

- Lewis Bernard, formerly a partner at Morgan Stanley, started Classroom Inc., which gives computers and computer instruction every year to inner-city children. Starting with nothing, he has developed a program that has provided several thousand computers to schools throughout the New York City area.

- Herb Granath, a creator of Monday Night Football and one of the leading forces behind the cable network ESPN, always has said, "It is time to give back." Herb has given back regularly to his church, to his job, to young people, and to countless others.

- Honeywell Inc. is one of the Minneapolis area's leading philanthropic institutions. In 1998 the company donated approximately $13.4 million to education, housing, and low-income neighborhoods. Local leaders hope that the company's recent merger with Allied Signal will not deplete its financial commitments to the area.

- Father Ted Hesburgh is one of the most accomplished educators of our time. He regularly works with inner-city young people and never takes credit for anything that he accomplishes.

Giving thanks is a way of acknowledging you're part of something bigger than yourself.

Beginnings of Humility

Showing gratitude to others is the very beginning of humility. It's far easier to find fault with others than it is to rejoice in their positive contributions, for in thanking people, you are acknowledging your own vulnerability and weaknesses.

Gratitude allows you to show appreciation for the shared power of accomplishment. When the president of the United States says thank you to his cabinet and staff, it's clear from the enormous responsibilities of his office that he is sharing the glory along with the credit. When companies give their CEOs special bonuses, they're recognizing these leaders for their special achievements as well as offering an incentive to continue their good work. They're also sending a message to their employees: "This person is doing a great job, and we trust him to keep the company successful. You can trust him, too."

The Importance of Trust

To depend on something or someone other than ourselves, we need to have trust. The Israelites had to learn to trust the hard way. Although the Lord had proved his commitment to his people in Egypt, trust would not come easy. Not only did the Lord send ten spectacular plagues to the Egyptian people, the Lord also parted the Red Sea when the Egyptians tried to recapture their slaves and provided food and drink in the barren desert. Wasn't that enough for the Israelites to realize that the Lord was on their side?

No. The Israelites were always falling back into mistrust. When Moses had been on Mount Sinai for more than forty days, they lost trust in him and in the Lord. They built a false god—a golden calf—to worship so that they would have visible evidence of someone or something that would take care of them.

Today, when followers lose trust in their leaders, they also seek a new one.

- In the United States, two presidents—Andrew Johnson and Bill Clinton—have been impeached due to lack of trust on the part of the people and the legislature. A third, Richard Nixon, resigned before impeachment hearings were initiated.

- In Moscow, President Boris Yeltsin faced numerous threats of impeachment by Parliament on charges that included waging illegal war, the breakup of the Soviet Union, the collapse of the military, the "genocide" of the Russian people, and even bringing Russia to ruin.

- In Israel, the people have the right to call for early elections when they distrust their leaders' intents and believe they are not performing the duties they were elected to perform.

In today's world, it's easy for a leader to lose our trust. How many CEOs have been criticized for, and even forced out of their jobs because of, poor management or fiscal irresponsibility?

Having a leader we can trust is necessary for our security and happiness. From the time we are children, we learn that being happy and secure makes it easier for us to reach our personal goals.

Today's leaders must recognize what gets in the way of their ability to establish trust among their followers. I know of many executives who are told by lawyers not to express gratitude, either by word or letter, to an employee. Such communication, they are told, can be a liability in a court of law should the company choose to fire that person later.

Promoting trust among workers is an equally important goal for managers and supervisors. It's easy for fellow workers to become suspicious of one another's actions. Employees who don't shoulder their share of the work aren't considered trustworthy. Others begin to resent them. If their work ethic doesn't improve, the morale of the company suffers.

An executive at General Electric once told me how one of the company's plants tried to develop more trust among its staff. The plant initiated a program called "Count on Me," in which workers agreed to be accessible to others in many areas of their jobs. The program worked. It fostered a level of trust among co-workers that resulted in higher levels of productivity at that plant than at any other.

It's not unusual for leaders themselves to lose trust. After the Hebrews arrived in the desert at Zin and camped at Kadesh, they became frightened by the lack of water. They demanded that Moses find them a spring. Moses took their demands to the Lord, who told him to gather the people at a rock and tell them that the Lord would turn the rock into flowing water. With that, Moses approached the rock and announced, "Hear now, ye rebels. Must we fetch you water out of this rock?" (Num. 20:10–11). When Moses struck the rock twice with his rod, enough water poured forth for the entire community.

Moses, however, had doubted that the Lord would come through with his promise and neglected to mention that the water was a gift from God. The people witnessed his moment of doubt. Because Moses' trust in the Lord wavered, the Lord banned him from entering the Promised Land. This condemnation of Moses was severe. But Moses had demonstrated a lack of trust before his followers that was tantamount to showing disbelief in his cause and in God.

> **Learning to trust and being
> trustworthy go hand in hand.**

Learning Thanksgiving

Many leaders of nations and religious organizations encourage gratitude as a means of unifying the people and keeping them focused on the underlying principles that solidify their society.

In an effort to encourage the Hebrews to show gratitude, the Lord instructed Moses to make thanksgiving a part of the people's daily lives. This was accomplished in large part by creating rituals—such as sacrificing animals before the tabernacle—that reminded the Israelites to give thanks to a higher power. "Three times in a year shall all thy males appear before the Lord thy God in the place which he shall choose; in the feast of unleavened bread, and in the feast of weeks, and in the feast of tabernacles; and they shall not appear before the Lord empty. Every man shall give as he is able, according to the blessing of the Lord thy God which he hath given thee" (Deut. 16:16–17).

The Israelites were slow learners, however. The Lord made them wander in the desert for forty years until they got it right.

Awe

By being capable of awe, we are closer to expressing gratitude.

Moses constantly evidenced his tremendous admiration for the Lord. When he received the Ten Commandments, he was filled with awe and spiritual ecstasy. The Bible calls this state "fallen down yet with open eyes" (Num. 24:4). Moses' gratitude to the Lord was never questioned.

Many people experience a feeling of awe when faced with the energy of an extraordinary leader.

Accepting Disappointment

Accepting disappointment prevents us from becoming ungrateful.

Moses was disappointed at not being allowed into the Promised Land, but this didn't stop him from continuing in his leadership role and teaching the Israelites how to lead a spiritually inspired life. Nor did it interfere with his ability to ensure a smooth leadership succession.

In a formal ceremony before his people, Moses honored Joshua as the new leader of the Israelites. Had he not been grateful for all the honors he himself had received from the Lord for leading the Israelites out of bondage, he might not have made the succession for Joshua so easy.

Many CEOs who are forced out of their positions of leadership, however, are not as magnanimous. Lee Iacocca tried to oust his successor, Robert Eaton, even though Iacocca himself had brought Eaton in from General Motors as his replacement designate. His behavior prompted one industry insider to remark, "Iacocca treats heirs apparent the way Henry VIII treated his wives. The longer he has to live with this guy, the longer he has to find fault with him." Had Iacocca been more highly evolved as a leader, he would have assisted in the transfer of power. Instead, he left a lasting impression as an ungrateful leader.

Many companies take special measures to ensure a smooth transition of leadership. When Baxter International Inc.'s CEO, Vernon Loucks, retired after eighteen years, the company's directors gave him a special stock-option grant for implementing a smooth transition. As Jill Carter, vice president of corporate communications, explained, "We absolutely wanted Vern to continue to work very closely with [his successor], our customers, government folks, and to continue as an active chairman."

Those with Gratitude

Gratitude seems to come naturally to some.

- The late comedian Danny Thomas was a high school dropout who wandered into show business through the back door of a burlesque house. Once bitten by the entertainment bug, he prayed to Saint Jude, the Roman Catholic patron saint of desperate situations, for his success and made a pledge: "Help me find my place in life, and I will build you a shrine where the poor and the helpless and the hopeless may come for comfort and aid." That very day he received a job offer and went on to have a successful career as a stand-up comic and Emmy Award-winning television star. In 1962 Thomas made good on his promise and established St. Jude Children's Research Hospital, the largest pediatric cancer research center in the world.

- Television superstar Oprah Winfrey never hesitates to express her thanks to those who paved the way to her success. "I have crossed over on the backs of Sojourner Truth and Harriet Tubman and Fannie Lou Hamer and Madame C. J. Walker," she has said, referring to African-American women who have succeeded in activism and commerce. "Because of them, I can now live the dream."

- The late Harvard Law School professor Phillip Areeda loved his job. First-year law students who found themselves in his classes would quake in their seats as he circled the room and put them on the spot with difficult cases to analyze. When he learned he had a terminal illness, Areeda decided to thank Harvard for the opportunity of teaching there. In his will, he bequeathed the school his estate, valued in excess of $5 million. It was one of the largest gifts the school had received in its 300-year history. Areeda was shocked by the amount of publicity his gift received in the press. He hardly thought the gesture was news-worthy; to him, turning over all his money to the law school in gratitude for the time he spent there seemed like a very natural thing to do. In his honor, Areeda now has a building at Harvard named after him.

- Named by the *Wall Street Journal* as a "just in time" CEO for his ability to save companies in serious financial and management trouble, Robert "Steve" Miller has been known for his ability to show grati-tude. Because of this, the media has treated him well and his staff has given their all for him.

Those Who Needed to Learn Gratitude

- Michael Milken, the former Drexel Burnham Lambert banker and millionaire, had to serve a prison term and battle prostate cancer before he learned a secret of happiness: Be thankful for what you have. During the 1980s, while he was at Drexel, he helped popularize "junk" bonds and served time for violating securities law. Upon his release, Milken became involved in business, educational projects, and charitable activi-ties. He has been one of the leading private donors to cancer research in the country. *Vanity Fair* has called him one of the most influential leaders of our times.

- A crack cocaine addict who lived in the crawl space beneath the platform of track 109 in Manhattan's Grand Central Station, Lee Stringer existed only for the next high, selling aluminum cans for cash to help support his habit. When he realized that the stick he was using to clean the resin from his crack pipe was actually a pencil, he began to write about his life and experiences. Stringer discovered that he had a gift for writing. He was so grateful that he was determined to protect it by getting clean. A contributing writer to *Street News,* a newspaper written by the homeless, he wrote a book, *Grand Central Winter: Stories from the Street,* which was published to high acclaim.

The Road to Gratitude

Developing an attitude of gratitude has awesome benefits. We enjoy inner peace. We don't envy our neighbor's new car. We like ourselves just as we are. We're thankful for all the hard knocks in life because they have taught us important lessons. Instead of judging or blaming others, we're more likely to help them out. But how do we get there? Here are some pointers on becoming more grateful.

 Find Someone Worse Off Than You
Offer to help him or her. If you've just lost a job and have two children, find someone in the same boat who has six children. Share your resources with that

person. You'll find that your own burden becomes lighter.

✓ List the Gifts Nature Has Given You

One woman I know made such a list. It included: good teeth/low dentist bills, health, pretty blue eyes, even disposition, able to fall asleep immediately, great singing voice, adept at math and computers, and genuine love of people. Once she made this list, she felt that she could never complain about anything again.

✓ Really Listen to Other People

By forgetting ourselves and becoming involved with others, we quickly realize that everyone has pain, disappointments, and squashed dreams.

✓ Stop Complaining!

Try calling a one-week moratorium on complaining and see how it feels to live complaint-free. For every slip, donate five dollars to a good cause.

> # "Thanks" is a small word that carries a big wallop.

6

Justice and Compassion

> The parents of three young boys were killed when their plane exploded over Colorado. When the boys' schoolmates requested that a memorial prayer service for the parents be held, the three boys were grateful, but the oldest asked for one more thing: "Can we also pray for the person who put that bomb on the plane?"

One of the most effective—and hardest—tasks a leader has is balancing justice with compassion. If an employee embezzles money, should he or she be fired? Or should the employee be given the chance, through therapy, to rehabilitate himself or herself? When this happened at a petroleum company, the CEO decided to be merciful. He had the employee pay back the money and get psychological help.

Many people agreed with his decision. But such decisions don't always work out so smoothly. Former President Gerald Ford received his share of criticism for pardoning the disgraced

Richard Nixon for his role in the Watergate scandal cover-up. Some reasoned that Ford wanted to preserve the dignity of the office of the presidency. Some suggested that he believed Nixon had suffered enough by resigning and that no further punishment was necessary. Others speculated that Ford was doing Nixon a political favor. Many Americans felt that Ford's actions prevented justice from being done.

The Call for Justice

Our desire for justice dates back to ancient times. During the eighteenth century B.C., the Babylonian king Hammurabi created a code of laws called the Code of Hammurabi. The quality usually most associated with the god from whom Hammurabi received the code—Shamash, the sun god—is justice.

Hammurabi's code—the earliest legal code known in its entirety—directed legal procedures and stated the penalties for unjust accusations, false testimony, and injustices committed by judges. It set laws concerning property rights, financial transactions, personal injury, and family rights. The code gave protection to all classes of Babylonian society and was considered humane for its time. In it, Hammurabi counseled his people: "Let any oppressed man who has a cause come into the presence of my statue as king of justice, and have the inscription on my stele read out, and hear my precious words, that my stele may make the case clear to him; may he understand his cause, and may his heart be set at ease!"

But while the laws of Hammurabi were long on justice, they were short on, if not devoid of, compassion. There was no room for excuses. Only the facts were considered. Based on a crude system of the biblical code "an eye for an eye," the punishment for breaking the laws usually was death. If one gave false testimony, for example, one was put to death. If a home fell down and killed a man, the builder was put to death; if a home fell down and killed the owner's son, the builder's son was put to death.

As in Hammurabi's and Moses' time, justice, in its simplest sense, usually means a blind or impartial application of the letter of the law. Modern man's sense of justice is often not that simple.

- In 1998, when Karla Faye Tucker was on death row in Texas, many people advocated that her death sentence be commuted. Among them were Pope John Paul II and the Protestant minister Tucker had married while imprisoned for the murder of two people. Tucker's supporters maintained that having embraced Christianity, become a "new woman," and demonstrated remorse, Tucker should be shown compassion. But Texas lawmakers decided that justice demanded Tucker die because she had murdered two innocent people and showed no remorse at the time for her actions. Her sentence—death by lethal injection—was ultimately carried out.

- In 1979 Stephen Fagan kidnapped his two young daughters from his ex-wife during what was supposed to be a weekend visit. He relocated them from Massachusetts to Florida, changed their names, and told them their mother had died in a car accident. Almost twenty years later, he was arrested after Massachusetts State Police received a tip that he was living in Florida. In a plea-bargain agreement, Fagan received a sentence of probation and a $100,000 fine, prompting legal experts to question whether prosecutors in the case had sent the wrong message by keeping Fagan from serving time in prison for kidnapping. Critics of the decision maintained that kidnapping is a serious offense, even if committed by a parent.

As times change, so does a society's understanding of justice. What was considered just in Moses' time would be called barbaric today. In the Book of Exodus one finds this example of an Israelite who was discovered working on the Sabbath, the day that commemorates the seventh day of creation and which the Ten Commandments prescribe as the day of rest:

"And while the children of Israel were in the wilderness, they found a man that gathered sticks upon the sabbath day. And they that found him gathering sticks brought him unto Moses and Aaron, and unto all the congregation. And they put him in ward, because it was not declared what should be done to him. And the Lord said unto Moses, The man shall be surely put to death: all the congregation shall stone him with stones without the camp. And all the congregation brought him without the camp, and stoned him with stones, and he died; as the Lord commanded Moses" (Num. 15: 32–36).

The Call for Compassion

Since Moses' time, the law gradually has offered more forgiveness. Forgiveness is a by-product of compassion.

Applying compassion means taking into account an almost infinite number of factors instead of just the facts. What if the person being judged is retarded, mentally ill, starving, from a broken home, in a jealous rage, or young and naïve? That's just the beginning of the list of possible mitigating circumstances that influence how we judge others. Bringing compassion into a court of law can be controversial, however.

- In the United States, youths who commit crimes are tried by a code of law that differs from the laws that apply to adults. The law utilizes the majority age— 18—as its measure for when an individual should be held accountable for his or her actions as an adult. For years, though, some states have waived the age limit and tried underage defendants as adults for serious crimes. Despite their youth, or their inability to distinguish right from wrong, or the amount of violence they see in the media, or the violent computer games they play, these states argue that violent youths deserve the same treatment as adults for the deaths of innocent people. Some states have even considered the death penalty for these teenagers.

- In a lawsuit concerning the 1998 Los Angeles murder-suicide of a woman who killed her husband, then herself, damages were sought by the woman's brother from the manufacturer of an antidepressant for the drug's effect on the woman's emotional state. The suit alleged that Pfizer Inc. downplayed the potential side effects—including violence and suicide—on certain individuals taking the drug.

Striking a Balance

Balancing justice with compassion is difficult. Not everyone agrees with the decisions that are made. Usually there are no clear right or wrong answers.

The balance of justice and compassion is affected by the times.

- As the United States swung from the liberal 1960s to the more conservative 1970s, many people began to feel less optimistic about society's ability to rehabilitate criminals and more aggressive about punishing criminals. As a society we became less compassionate. In 1976 the death penalty was reinstated. Today the federal government and thirty-nine states incorporate the death penalty in their rulings.

- Fifty years after the Nazis succeeded in murdering more than six million European Jews, claims are being brought by Holocaust survivors and their families against insurance firms that failed to honor policies of those whose family members died in the Holocaust; banks that refused to allow family members to withdraw money deposited by their deceased relatives; and companies that utilized slave labor. Such cases are representative of the recent international interest in global settlements of Holocaust claims.

- Modern scientific research on DNA can help legislators determine the guilt or innocence of a suspect. Through the application of such research, many inmates, including some on death row, have been proven innocent of crimes they were accused of committing.

Unlike in Hammurabi's time, Moses' exacting and explicit law on issues such as the death penalty have made it difficult for our leaders to balance justice and compassion. Today those who believe murderers should not be rehabilitated are struggling with the issue of error—is the wrong person being executed? Experts have acknowledged that since the death penalty was reinstated in 1976, seventy-five people on death row have been proven innocent. How do our leaders rectify the errors of a legal system that can send innocent people to their deaths?

Some of the greatest compassion and forgiveness in death penalty cases have been demonstrated by the families of murder victims. Some of these families, through Murder Victims' Families for Reconciliation (MVR), conduct "journeys of hope" in different states, seeking to abolish the death penalty. Such a group would have been unimaginable in Moses' day.

This raises an intriguing question for America's CEOs who so often play a role in forming our national ethic. Having lost the notion of rehabilitation, have some of today's corporate leaders lost the value of forgiveness and recovery?

Moses the Lawgiver

In spite of the stern aspects of Mosaic law, the leader of the Israelites sometimes balanced the letter of God's law with the spirit of forgiveness. He knew when justice should prevail and when it should be tempered with mercy. This ability to balance justice and compassion helped Moses to become a great, perhaps the greatest, lawgiver.

Applying the Law
Moses took the laws the Lord set down and presented them to the people. He explained where there was ambiguity and made judgments based on those laws.

Creating a Legal Organization
At first, Moses acted as legislator and judge, administering the laws of the Lord all by himself. When the job became too much for one person to handle, he followed the perceptive suggestions of his father-in-

law, Jethro, and passed some of his authority to others in the community, creating a prototype of a modern legal organization. Those cases that were too difficult for lower-ranking judges to settle were turned over to higher-ranking judges. Moses told his judicial recruits: "I charged your judges at that time, saying: 'Hear the causes between your brethren, and judge righteously between every man and his brother, and the stranger that is with him'" (Deut. 1:16).

The Ten Commandments

Moses was committed to bringing the law to his people. He withstood forty days on Mount Sinai before the Lord was ready to release the Ten Commandments. After he smashed the original tablets, Moses went back up the mountain to receive them from the Lord again.

The Ten Commandments were considered sacred. They became the foundation of Jewish law, which details man's obligation both to the Lord and to other human beings.

The law gave the Israelites an identity. Because they all agreed to obey certain laws, they were one people. The United States Constitution serves a similar role in that it gives Americans a clear notion of what they believe in. The biblical Commandments, the American Constitution, and English Common Law, interestingly, are the basis for every corporate code of ethics.

Compassion for His People

Moses understood his people's suffering. He didn't punish them for complaining. Some ancient leaders would have quieted their followers by executing a few to serve as an example. To them, that would have constituted "justice." One CEO of an aerospace firm made it a practice to fire one subordinate whenever his employees objected to their working conditions. After each firing, the complaints stopped; the employees learned to keep their grievances to themselves.

Many times, Moses made sure the Lord didn't punish the people excessively. In the desert, when the Israelites made the golden calf and broke the law concerning worshiping idols, Moses knew the Lord wanted to destroy all the people. He offered to be punished in their place. Jewish law does not recognize surrogates, however; only the people can make up for their sins. Because of this, the Lord refused to administer punishment to the Israelites vicariously. But Moses pleaded so intently that the Lord eventually backed down from his original plan of punishment. Only those guilty of participating in making and worshiping the idol were killed.

Why was Moses compassionate? Maybe he understood that human behavior is universal in its tendency to glorify the past—when graven images were the rule—and disparage the present. More important, Moses identified with the people. He didn't perceive himself as set apart. He asked the Lord to "pardon our iniquity and our sin" (Exod. 34:9). Moses considered himself as much a sinner as the rest of the Israelites.

Moses as a Role Model

It was also in the desert that the Lord revealed to Moses the merciful side of his nature. If the people repented, the Lord was ready to show mercy. That helped Moses enormously. At times the Lord was very stern, but the Lord could be persuaded to forgive. The Lord was a good role model. If the Lord could forgive, so could Moses.

There are elements of Moses as a role model in the following leaders.

- Although his primary concern was maintaining the unity of the United States, Abraham Lincoln's opposition to slavery during the Civil War was based on his belief in the legal and moral principles on which the country was founded—particularly those expressed in the Declaration of Independence—and in the premise that slavery was morally, socially, and politically wrong. Lincoln's compassion for the slaves and his commitment to free them resulted in the enactment of the Emancipation Proclamation, which guaranteed the slaves their freedom and underscored their entitlement as citizens to all legal rights.

- Although he led the United States in the war against the Japanese during World War II, General Douglas MacArthur became a leader in America's postwar effort to reform and democratize Japan. His efforts to help in the legal and economic rebuilding of the country made him a hero to many Japanese. MacArthur's compassion for his enemies allowed him to pave the way for economic prosperity and legal stability for the Japanese, as well as a constructive role for Japan in the world arena.

- Václav Havel, the president of the Czech Republic, brought democratic reform to a country once dominated by communism. A champion of the people, he emerged as a leader who worked to redefine his country's politics as well as the role of the politician. "A politician," he said, "must become a person again, someone who trusts not only a scientific representation and analysis of the world, but also the world itself. He must not only believe in sociological statistics, but in real people. He must not only trust an objective interpretation of reality, but also its soul."

- Our greatest lawgivers are those who serve on the Supreme Court, who are entrusted with the duty of determining which laws are just. Although justice may be an abstract principle to some, the Supreme Court justice tries to formulate the law in such a way that it can be applied fairly to all members of society, not just those with the means to be protected by it. In the Miranda case, for example, the Court decreed that all criminal suspects are entitled to be warned of their rights to remain silent and to counsel before they are interrogated.

All of us, whether or not we're leaders, struggle to balance justice and compassion. Here are just a handful of examples.

- David Kaczynski, brother of Theodore Kaczynski, the Unabomber, had to define for himself what was justice and what was compassion. After reading the anonymous Unabomber's published manifesto against technology, David realized it was probably his brother who was sending bombs through the mail and maiming or killing those whose philosophies he violently opposed. David wanted to stop further deaths, but he also wanted to understand his brother and remain loyal to him. After a tremendous amount of soul searching, he reported his suspicions to the authorities. Eventually, Theodore escaped the death penalty, but David may always wonder if he was truly successful in striking a balance.

- When popular columnist Mike Barnicle was accused of misrepresenting material for his column, the editors of the *Boston Globe* had to weigh justice with compassion. Some critics said that Barnicle should be fired for violating the canons of journalism and misleading readers; that was justice. Others campaigned for forgiveness based on Barnicle's reputation and his admission of his own guilt; that was compassion. After admitting that he had recycled stories he had heard from others and had published them without verifying them, Barnicle was suspended. He later resigned, leaving many to question whether a well-meaning person's career should be sacrificed on the altar of professional ethics.

- Each year, *Working Mother* magazine publishes its list of the "100 Best Companies for Working Mothers," companies that most successfully support the attempt by female employees to balance work and family issues. Many organizations have come under fire for their inability to combine compassion for their employees with company policies. Companies that willingly honor the 1993 Family and Medical Leave Act—which entitles employees to parental leave for newborns and adopted children as well as time away from the office for taking care of ill, aging parents—are leaders in compassion.

- A Roman Catholic nun who became active in counseling inmates on death row in Louisiana's Angola Prison, Sister Helen Prejean has had to balance her compassion for two men on death row with her compassion for the relatives of their murder victims. "The Church must stand on both sides of the Cross. It must stand behind everyone who is hurting, and that includes death row inmates and victims' families," she has explained. Sister Prejean often speaks out against the death penalty, abhorring any act of murder. "Human beings are not disposable waste. . . . Who are we to say human life is irredeemable?"

Finding a Balance

As in Moses' day, so many of the issues we face today emerge because of a clash between justice and compassion.

- Was it just for the Roman Catholic Church to grant Congressman Joseph Kennedy an annulment of his long-term first marriage? Where was the Church's compassion for his first wife and their grown children?

- Is it just for the courts to impose the maximum penalty on teenagers who murder their newborns, or should society show compassion for its youth?

- Is it just for our presidents to engage in controversial acts of clemency, such as President Ford's pardon of Richard Nixon; President Nixon's commuting of James Hoffa's racketeering sentence; President Clinton's conditional pardon of Puerto Rican militants; or

President Carter's commuting of Patricia Hearst's bank robbery sentence?

Today's society is in dire need of balancing justice with compassion. As individuals, we can try the following.

✔ **Put Yourself in Someone Else's Shoes**
Mahatma Gandhi told a Hindu man who had killed a Muslim that to make restitution, he should adopt a Muslim child and raise that child as a Muslim. Only by understanding someone else's perspective can we make just decisions with compassion.

✔ **Really Know What the Issue Is**
It's easy to get information about a variety of issues. Go online, read books and magazines, watch TV news and opinion shows. Knowing all sides of an issue helps us formulate our own ideas about justice.

✔ **Admit Your Blind Spots**
Not everyone is impartial about every issue. Our own experiences can cause blind spots in our vision, affecting our ability to see the issues clearly. If we walked five miles to school every day in the snow when we were young, we might not have much compassion today for a school district that wants to raise funds for new school buses. If we're barely making a living wage, we might not have compassion for highly paid union workers or baseball players who are on strike for better wages.

✔ **Know Your Core Values**
We all need core beliefs, whether they are about murder, religion, education, or parenting. Once we're clear about our core values, the rest should fall into place.

We should be able to make the decisions that are true to our values.

✓ Support Character Education

Ethics and building moral character—whether at home or school or in your church, synagogue, or mosque—are important topics to teach our children. Organizations such as Character Education Partnership have been helping to ensure that the next generation learns and applies morals and ethics to their lives and to society.

> # Justice without mercy is the legal system of barbarians.

7

Being the Critic

For about thirty years, a minister led a vibrant congregation in a small town in the Midwest. He was like an institution to the people who flocked to him whenever there was a joyful or sorrowful occasion.

Then the minister's health began to fail, and he wasn't able to perform his job. Many left his church and joined other congregations. As his congregation dwindled in number, the minister evaluated his situation and his ability to lead his parishioners. Reluctantly, he came to a decision.

One Sunday, he loaded everyone onto buses and took them to another minister's church. Before they got off the buses, he said: "I had to become critical of myself. What I see is an old, sick man. You deserve better. That's why I want you to join this minister's church."

The minister and his congregation attended the service at the new church. There wasn't a dry eye in the house. Everyone was aware that the minister had put the needs of the congregation ahead of his own.

Criticism, whether you give it to yourself or receive it from others, is a powerful tool. By putting his own ego aside, the ailing minister in the story above was able to evaluate his potential and realistically determine his effectiveness as a leader. In a sense, he fired himself and appointed a new shepherd for his followers.

When he reached a very old age, Moses also realized he could no longer lead and passed the scepter to Joshua. "And Moses went and spake these words unto all Israel. . . . I can no more go out and come in: also the Lord hath said unto me, Thou shalt not go over this Jordan" (Deut. 31:1–2). For many decades, Moses had led his people toward the goal of the Promised Land. Yet even when it was in his sight, he was wise enough to accept the inevitable.

For Moses and the minister, what looks like resignation was actually a powerful sign of leadership. Stepping down and providing a successor ensures that the people continued working toward their goal. It allows leaders the opportunity to explore other pursuits.

Meg Whitman left a successful career at a toy company in Boston to run an unknown online auction house in San Jose, California. Despite her initial reluctance to relocate her family and enter the uncharted world of e-commerce, Whitman recognized an opportunity for leadership. "I thought something was very right here. They had touched a consumer nerve." As chief executive of Ebay, Inc. she became a leading force in bringing conventional management experience to the Web.

Whether you're a CEO, a manager, or a team leader, self-awareness is empowering.

His Own Best Critic

Moses was constantly reexamining his own performance. Early on he informed the Lord that he wasn't a good speaker. The Lord assigned Moses' brother, Aaron, to speak for him.

Through self-criticism, Moses identified a weakness and opened it up to discussion. By doing so, he paved the way for a solution and kept intact the Lord's plan to lead the Hebrew slaves to freedom. Likewise, an employee who is self-critical and identifies a weakness makes it possible for others to help him get the job done and for the company to reach its objectives.

Many leaders are able to evaluate themselves and strive to be better. William R. Johnson, CEO of H. J. Heinz Co., claims he is harder on himself than his critics are. "At the end of the day, the grade I give myself will always be lower than the one I received in the marketplace or from the board, or people working for me."

Successful executives review their actions and analyze what they could have done better. A man I'll call Robert worked with me years ago for a large corporation. A few times a day Robert silently reviewed how things were going. He examined what he did right and what he did wrong. If he realized that he had been abrupt with me or if he hadn't really listened, he'd tell me he was sorry. He usually avoided making that same mistake again. Robert had a sense of peace we all admired.

> ## Criticizing ourselves
> ## gives us mastery over ourselves.

Too many people get so caught up in their own egos that they cannot recognize signs of failure. They limit the potential for self-improvement and the realization of their goals.

- Henry Kissinger's stubborn position in prolonging the Vietnam War, evidenced in his repetition of the refrain "Peace with Honor," added to the loss of life suffered by American and Vietnamese soldiers. The former Secretary of State could neither admit to the failure of his policy nor accept the fact that America would not win the war.

- Hillary Clinton failed to get Congress to enact comprehensive health care reform. She didn't recognize that she lacked public support for the kinds of radical reform measures she was proposing. Her conviction that she knew better than others what would be best for the American people not only was responsible for her own and the Clinton administration's loss of credibility, but also paved the way for the Republican victory in the House of Representatives during the 1994 congressional elections.

The Art of Self-criticism

Effective leaders use self-criticism as a tool for change and for keeping themselves and their followers on the right track. Executives of Barnes & Noble drew up a plan to acquire Ingram Book Group, the nation's largest book wholesaler, but the Federal Trade Commission concluded that the bookseller's attempt violated antitrust law. However, even before the FTC's decision, leaders of Barnes & Noble had examined the liabilities in their acquisi-

tion plan and anticipated the criticism of others. They had prepared an alternate plan for cost-efficient distribution and product delivery. Being self-critical allowed them to keep their focus
on the company's goals.

The art of self-criticism entails some essential skills.

 ### Accept Yourself as Less Than Divine

This is hard for many successful people. They see
themselves as being larger than life and would like to
believe that they're more than human. We can accept
our place in the universe by celebrating what's best
about ourselves. That's why watching the Olympics or
reading the history of medicine is so thrilling. We can
say: "One of us really did this." If we accept our own
humanity, our faults no longer seem so big and bad.

 ### Like Yourself

If we like ourselves, we'll want to help ourselves. We'll
want to know our bad traits as well as our good traits
so that we can make our experiences positive forces in
our lives. Practicing objective self-love can make even
the negative side of ourselves understandable and thus
open to change.

 ### Make Time for Introspection

Success in the information age demands that we constantly keep ingesting data from the Internet, from
newspapers, from television and radio, and from con-
versations. But to know ourselves better, we need to
break away and spend time alone. By having the time
to examine our conscience, we can take an inventory
of our faults. If one day's inventory tells us we've been
impatient with people four times that day, we know
we have a behavioral pattern that needs to be broken.

Examining ourselves helps us keep our peace of mind and preserves our relationships with others.

✓ **Forgive Yourself**

It's unrealistic to consider ourselves so bad that we can't be forgiven. To forgive ourselves means moving beyond decisions that have caused pain or failure. It means acknowledging an error and learning from the mistake. Those of us who never learn self-forgiveness become wooden and live unhappy lives.

Without self-criticism, we can't grow, either in our personal lives or in our careers. Many managers can use the principle of self-criticism to their advantage: by managing themselves, they can more effectively manage their team.

Self-criticism leads to:

- self-awareness
- humility
- an open mind
- recognition of one's faults
- self-forgiveness

Criticism from Others

Criticism from others helps us see what we can't see on our own. Some leaders hire personal coaches to be their extra pair of eyes. Some find mentors—as they did when they were just starting out. Others join spiritual groups to gain insight about themselves. Whatever the method, seeking criticism is a route to self-improvement.

One-time television personality Sally Quinn failed at her news anchor job because no one gave her constructive criticism about how she was presenting herself on camera. An untrained amateur, she was rushed on the air by a network that hadn't given a thought to her preparation. She didn't know she should be "punching" certain words. She didn't know how to read a TelePrompTer. Her ad-libbed comments were not toned down. After only five months on "The CBS Morning News," she quit the program to return to newspaper reporting.

There may, however, be a danger in too much criticism. The late singer Judy Garland received plenty of constructive criticism, and it may have been too much. Under the pressure, she succumbed to substance abuse. It ended her career—and her life.

When Moses was leading his followers toward the land of Canaan, he was constantly being judged by the Lord and his people. Although the Lord was pleased with Moses' performance most of the time, whenever he was not, he did not hesitate to criticize.

This behavior teaches us two things. First, even the most perfect of bosses must answer to someone and is not above having his or her performance critiqued. Second, to react defensively to such appraisal is to forget the value of criticism. None of us is perfect and all of us can improve.

> # No one, not even a leader, is exempt from performance evaluation.

Seeking Feedback

Receiving criticism from others means getting feedback from outside ourselves. Moses listened carefully to his father-in-law Jethro's advice on delegating the dispensing of justice to the Israelites. As an outsider, Jethro could see the pitfalls of Moses' leadership. He had objectivity and could offer the right solution.

One way companies receive the benefits of outside help is by hiring consultants or bringing in CEOs from other firms.

- When New Age Electronics Inc., a national distributor of brand-name office products for small businesses, needed to create a new infrastructure to handle its growth, the company hired a consulting firm specializing in workouts, turnarounds, and exit strategies. With the consultant's help, New Age was able to identify its weaknesses and strengths and plan a strategy to help manage the company's growth. "We learned that we focused very well in handling specific projects for specific customers, but we didn't run as a team," a New Age executive remarked. The consultant helped refine every aspect of the company's management, and the company's revenue jumped from $56 million in 1995 to $433 million in 1998. "We could do pretty much anything we wanted, because the company is running on all cylinders," said the executive.

- CEO Louis V. Gerstner Jr. came to a floundering IBM and put a torch to most of its old corporate culture. He turned the company around. As an outsider, he could be critical enough to do what an insider could not.

- For only the second time in its 146-year history, Levi Strauss & Company hired a CEO from outside its own ranks. In its appointment of Pepsi-Cola North America CEO Philip A. Marineau, Levi Strauss sought to increase its shrinking market share and revitalize its brand of blue jeans by hiring an executive with experience in consumer products instead of fashion.

Moses himself can be viewed as an outsider. A Hebrew by birth, he was raised as an Egyptian but felt like "a stranger in a strange land." He had married a Midian woman, a foreigner. At the time he became leader of the Hebrew slaves, he wasn't entirely comfortable with who he was or his Jewish heritage. He had to come up with an identity of his own. This gave him an advantage: he became self-aware in a way that the other Hebrews weren't. This put him in a good position to help the Israelites learn new aspects of their religion.

Whether we bring in a third party to help resolve family or business disputes or to help us redefine and refocus our company, seeking feedback can alter the way we see and behave.

Criticism as Revolution

Throughout history men and women have used criticism to change the way they live. Moses was critical of how the Egyptians treated the Hebrews. His belief that the Hebrews should be free to leave Egypt and be allowed to worship their Lord brought enormous change to both the Israelites and Egyptian society.

Many have learned from Moses' example.

- The American patriots were critical of how they were being ruled by the English. They rebelled against the government of King George III for taxation without representation. Their criticism sparked and fed the fire for independence.

- In 1989 Chinese students rallied in Tiananmen Square to protest their concerns about inflation, academic freedom, government corruption, freedom of the press, and democratic reform. Their ill-fated rebellion, during which hundreds were killed by the Chinese military, led to some gains in Chinese society. Students have been granted access to books criticizing socialism. The people have opportunities for better jobs, as well as some restricted freedom to criticize Communist Party policies and associate with the Chinese Democratic Party. Although the democratic movement in China is still restrained, there is somewhat more political openness in the urban and rural areas.

History's major revolutions, including the American and the Russian revolutions, were fueled by criticism of the status quo. Revolutions in health care, communication, business, religion, and legal and social reforms all began with people who were not satisfied with how things were being done.

- A Methodist minister named William Booth became critical of his religion when it failed to provide shelter for the hungry and the homeless. Recognizing that spiritual needs were linked with material ones, he founded the Salvation Army in 1865.

- In the 1900s suffragists fought to win the vote for women in America. Adapting the words of British activist Emmeline Pethick-Lawrence—"The only life worth living is a fighting life"—they worked tirelessly to bring women into the political arena.

- Moctesuma Esparza was one of the student leaders in the 1970s Chicano rights movement. Jailed and forced to go underground for his activities against institutional racism, Esparza became a successful Latino television and film producer, paving the way for other minority men and women to break into the entertainment industry.

- Harvard Law School professor Alan Dershowitz was openly critical of the law and the practices of lawyers in the courtroom. He set about to reform the field. Taking radical approaches to defend clients, he has given hope, directly or indirectly, to everyone, from those in mental hospitals to the overprivileged.

Free Will

We all make choices. Sometimes, however, we worry that being criticized will interfere with our ability to make choices, because we won't feel as open to explore our true potential. In fact, the opposite is true. Effective criticism works to keep us from wasting time on less efficient behavior and instead spotlights the talents in which our true potential lies.

Moses was critical of the Israelites. He believed they made choices in how they behaved. He used criticism as a tool to help guide those choices and was constantly moving the Israelites toward a more reasonable and God-fearing life on their way to the Promised Land.

Moses encouraged the people to take responsibility for their actions, even in extreme or crisis situations. He knew circumstances alone were not enough to justify behaving in ways that went against the Lord's teachings. Whether they were low on food and water or fighting an enemy army in the desert, Moses was quick to criticize when the people lost control of themselves.

Thus emerges an important leadership principle: Improvement is the by-product of criticism. Leaders who criticize place faith in their followers' ability to rise to the expected standards.

In many organizations, it's the employees with the highest potential who receive the most active criticism. This is the most flattering form of mentoring. Those employees who are perceived as just passing the time aren't nurtured. Their ability to move the company forward is questioned. When I worked for a large firm, if we weren't being hammered with criticism, we weren't on our way up.

Being critical, therefore, is a constructive way to bring out the potential of others. Parents wouldn't correct their children's manners or comment on their study habits if they didn't believe their children could do better.

Criticism is a way of helping mankind improve its behavior.

Knowledge Is Power

Moses knew his people well. He had plenty to criticize. For one thing, the people had short memories. No sooner had the Lord provided water in the desert than they began to worry about having enough to eat. When they received food, they wanted variety in their diet. Their trust in the Lord was shaky.

Moses chastised the Israelites for their lack of faith, but he never stopped believing in them. Because of that, he never stopped actively criticizing them. He knew they were capable of growth and demanded that they reach their potential. Annie Sullivan, Helen Keller's teacher, believed that the blind and deaf could function in society. That's why she was so hard on Helen. She knew the little girl could succeed.

Knowledge means power. Our leaders in business, in our schools, and in our society would make greater contributions by learning more about themselves and their followers.

Moses knew himself well. He realized he was not the perfect leader and took responsibility for his part in the failings of the Israelites. When the people acted up, he was the first to go to the Lord and ask forgiveness for them. Being acutely aware of his own imperfections, he placed a value on forgiveness. He knew that he was just another Israelite—with the mission to lead.

Like Moses, those who have been the most effective in their criticism understand human nature. They're realistic about who we mortals are.

- Hamish Maxwell, the former chair and CEO of Philip Morris, assumed leadership of the company at a crossroads in its history. He acquired a number of companies. When he discovered that not all of them were performing satisfactorily, he slowly and deliberately helped the companies' underachievers measure up. Candid in his criticism but generous in his praise and rewards, Maxwell molded the family of Philip Morris companies into a model of management excellence.

- When he was mayor of New York City, Ed Koch never had any illusions about people. He saw them for who they were. After a homeless woman made headlines by insisting on her rights to housing, medical care, and welfare benefits, she was invited to appear at Harvard Law School. Koch was critical of making this woman a celebrity. Knowing that her basic nature would not change regardless of the benefits she received, he predicted that after the woman received her fifteen minutes of fame, she would return to the streets. She did. Because of his handle on human nature, Koch didn't waste city resources on causes that wouldn't work.

Becoming a Good Critic

The ability to criticize is a great gift if it's done right. Handled well and channeled into constructive activities, it is one of the most powerful forces in the history of humankind. Criticism from a superior gives employees trust and confidence that their leader can show them how to improve.

We've all had a teacher, coach, or parent who came down on us in such a brutal manner that we still haven't recovered. When she was a teenager, Emme, the large-size supermodel, was criticized by her stepfather for her weight. He would circle the fat on her body with a Magic Marker. Luckily, Emme overcame that early obstacle to self-esteem. Today, at 5'11" and 185 pounds, she earns $5,000 a day as a top Ford fashion model.

If we want to help other people grow, the way Moses helped the Israelites become stronger, we have to know how to deliver criticism in the right ways. Here are some tips.

✓ Don't Underestimate Sensitivity

Tough men and women might not show their emotions, but that doesn't mean they don't have feelings at all. I remember having lunch with a second-year student at a top business school. We talked about a certain company's brand names. He shared with me what he thought about them, and I corrected him, perhaps harshly, about the image those brand names communicated. He didn't say much for the rest of our lunch. Later I discovered that this man disliked me, and his feelings toward me continue to this day. We're all fragile. Perhaps before we approach someone else with constructive criticism, we can run our ideas by a third party. An objective person can point out our insensitivity.

✓ Make Sure Your Criticism Will Be Helpful

At Seton Hill College, English instructor Sister Miriam Jane told a student writer that her work was "too cute." Maybe the timing was right. Maybe the student was ready to hear the criticism. Whatever the reason, the student started writing with more depth and went on to become a successful business writer.

The timing for objective criticism is usually right when people are in a crisis or when they reach bottom. They have little to lose in giving up a treasured illusion. A probation officer in Detroit told me that when people are in a crisis, they'll not only hear advice, but also aggressively seek it out. Yet in some cases, the reverse also can be true: people can be more receptive to hearing criticism when they're riding high. As every boss knows, when workers are at the top of their game, they're often more receptive to criticism.

> ## Criticism that isn't helpful has no place in human relationships. If what you are about to say won't be helpful, shelve it until another time.

✔ **Include Yourself among the Usual Suspects**
Identifying with others is the spoonful of sugar that helps the criticism go down. I'm most helpful to my new employees when I tell them about similar problems I had when I was starting out. Identifying with them takes a lot of the sting out of the criticism. At the University of Michigan, a political science professor was counseling a first-year graduate student who wasn't doing well in the class. The professor told the student his own story: how he had enrolled in law school, done poorly, and, realizing it was a bad fit, transferred to graduate school to study political sci-

ence. The student got the message that maybe he should consider another line of study.

✓ **Walk the Walk**

Avoid giving criticism that you yourself aren't willing to follow. This is particularly difficult for parents. If we're concerned about our child's weight, what are we doing with that bag of Doritos in our lap? Just because we haven't been hired by a client or don't have a boss looking over our shoulder doesn't mean we can pretend to be "off-stage" when delivering criticism at home. If we can't walk the walk, we have no right to be in the business of criticism.

✓ **Be Prepared to Be Wrong**

Offering criticism is a risk. No one is right all the time. I once told a man that he belonged in a corporation, not an ad agency. I felt that an ad agency was too chaotic for him. He ignored my advice and went on to become a big name in New York advertising. I was wrong and congratulated him for having the self-confidence to go his own way. How many people probably told Microsoft Corp.'s Bill Gates that he should stay at Harvard and finish his college education? Or Gerry Greenwald that he should not leave a secure job at Ford to work at the bankrupt Chrysler? Or Roseanne that she might not be attractive enough to make it in television? If our criticism turns out to be wrong, we should say we're sorry—and mean it.

It's How You Say It

Sometimes it's how we deliver the message that counts. Anger, disappointment, sarcasm, ridicule—these are all ingredients for disaster. We have a better chance of getting our message through by using other methods.

✓ **Show Humor**

Laughter is contagious. It lightens our mood. Using humor to drive a point home takes the edge off of criticism.

On his successful television series, comedian Jerry Seinfeld provided a humorous look into the lives of self-involved people. By holding a mirror up to the narcissism of our age, Seinfeld showed us all how we come across when we discuss our emotional aches and pains.

When he was vice president, Dan Quayle bore the brunt of political humor. When he launched his campaign for the Republican presidential nomination for the year 2000, he saw the humor directed his way as an indication that he was a serious political contender. Whether or not he succeeds as a politician, he has learned to use humor to set his own political agenda.

When Italian comedic actor and director Roberto Benigni accepted his Oscar for Best Actor for his film *Life Is Beautiful,* he joked, "I thank my parents for the gift of poverty." Benigni wasn't only being funny. In addition to learning the value of money and what it takes to be a success, poverty taught him about humility and caring. He took these lessons with him when he joined comedy and tragedy in his poignant film about the effects of the German invasion of Europe—and the Holocaust that followed—on a loving family.

✔ Issue Warnings

Moses continually issued warnings to the Israelites to keep them from behavior that was not holy. He told them, for example, that the fruits of the Promised Land and its cisterns, houses, and cities were gifts from God. He said, "Beware lest thou forget the Lord, who brought thee forth out of the land of Egypt, from the house of bondage" (Deut. 6:12). Moses' warning was critical of the Israelites' typical behavior, namely, being ungrateful.

✔ Tell Stories

Jesus, a student of the Mosaic books, gave criticism through the use of parables. Framing advice in short stories helped people accept his messages. The English novelist Charles Dickens used his ability as a storyteller to criticize humankind's inhumanity in Victorian England. His own youthful experiences in a debtor's prison and his work in a blacksmith's shop shaped his sympathies and found their way into his novels through such immortal characters as David Copperfield, Oliver Twist, and the Artful Dodger. The world paid attention to Dickens's gospel. His tale *A Christmas Carol*, about spiritual rebirth, is still a classic.

✔ Reinforce the Message

Because the Israelites had short memories, Moses used the technique of constant repetition. He knew if he said something just once, the people wouldn't "get it." Some leaders today call this "staying on message." In ancient Greek literature this meant repetition through refrains, such as in the text of Homer's *Iliad*. During the Renaissance, it meant using visuals that reinforced a lesson. The stained-glass windows in churches, for example, tell the story of the Old and New Testaments.

Moses' message was clear: Even though they were "chosen," the Israelites could blow their opportunity by believing that they deserved blessings they had not earned. Even as he was dying, he reminded the Hebrews once more of the choice they had. "I command thee this day to love the Lord thy God, to walk in his ways, and to keep his commandments and his statutes and his judgments, that thou mayest live and multiply: and the Lord thy God shall bless thee in the land whither thou goest to possess it. But if thine heart turn away, so that thou wilt not hear, but shalt be drawn away, and worship other gods, and serve them; I denounce unto you this day, that ye shall surely perish, and that ye shall not prolong your days upon the land, whither thou passest over Jordan to go to possess it" (Deut. 30: 16–18).

Another of Moses' oft-repeated messages was that of unity. Moses taught the people that they should be unified in the love of the Lord. Over and over again, they were told, "The Lord our God is one Lord. And thou shalt love the Lord thy God with all thine heart, and with all thy soul, and with all thy might" (Deut. 6:4–5). Unity was imperative for the survival of the Israelites. If the people were divided, they couldn't fight their enemies.

The importance of unity is a concept that has significance in today's world. We need unity to pass laws. Businesses need the talent and expertise of many people just to stay head-to-head with their competitors. In today's world of mergers and globalization, no one person or company can do everything.

> **Business leaders who stress unity
> help to build and reinforce
> a focus that keeps their followers
> moving in a common direction.**

✓ **Mete Out Punishment**

Moses was aware that being a leader means not just being the good guy. He used threats. The Lord provided a clear set of punishments. In this, the Jewish religion is quite legalistic. If you do X, Y is highly likely to happen. When Moses warned the people about harboring evil in their hearts or becoming self-righteous, he also warned of predictable punishment. Such sinners, he declared, will be ostracized from the group and cursed, and in some cases they were ordered slain—the edict of an angry God.

For years those who theorized about motivation claimed that punishment was a bad way to reinforce behavior. We began to rely more and more on the carrot, or positive reinforcement. Being critical was out; encouragement was in. We couldn't criticize a student's composition for weak organization; we had to find other aspects of it that could be praised.

Then common sense set in. As a former chief financial officer of a top corporation in control technology stated, a firing can send a powerful message. Criticism with punishment *can* work.

In human relationships and careers, criticism is a risky proposition. It can blow up in our faces. It can hurt others. Or it can work and help those we care about, including ourselves, reach our potential.

**Criticism delivered
in a caring way
can change a life.**

8

In Hard Times

> Mihajlo Mihajlov was a political prisoner in Yugoslavia. In his book Underground Notes, *he described what it was like living through hard times. He observed that when prisoners had to choose between saving their soul or saving their body, those who tried to protect their body lost everything—including their sense of self-worth. However, Mihajlov said, those who were determined to save their soul felt peace, dignity, and strength.*

Whether we lead a family or a country, we all encounter hard times. For a leader, these are the times that truly test our abilities, our commitments, our beliefs. They force us to be inventive, to break out of our comfort zone, to discover strengths we didn't know we had.

- As first lady, Hillary Rodham Clinton weathered the failure of her health care reform program, accusations in the Whitewater and the 1996 campaign finance scandals, and her husband's internationally publicized affair with the young White House intern Monica Lewinsky. Through it all, she carried herself with strength and dignity. In the summer of 1999, she announced her intention to explore running for the United States Senate from New York. She not only made it through the hard times, but also began to forge her own political identity.

- Pramoedya Ananta Toer, Indonesia's greatest modern writer, suffered for three decades under the military regime of President Suharto. A leftist and government critic, he lost his hearing during a struggle with the military police. He was later arrested without charge and imprisoned for fourteen years, some of which was spent at the island of Buru, a remote penal colony, where he composed in his head some of his best-known novels. On Human Rights Day in 1992 he liberated himself from house arrest simply by walking out onto the street. At 74, he published his memoir, *The Mute's Soliloquy,* documenting the mental and spiritual resistance he was able to bring forth during his imprisonment in Buru. Pramoedya's example teaches us about overcoming great adversity while maintaining dignity and a sense of duty to others.

Hard Times in History

Let's look at some difficult times in the twentieth century. Hopefully we've been able to learn from them.

The Great Depression

An Eastern European immigrant once told me how she and her family had come to America in hopes of greater economic opportunity. Instead they ran into a wall called the Great Depression—a breakdown of our financial institutions that plunged the country into economic chaos.

Few emerged unscathed. Families that had never known a hungry night were reduced to standing in bread lines and soup kitchens. Some wealthy citizens lost everything; some committed suicide. President Herbert Hoover's promise of a "chicken in every pot" was ridiculed in open demonstrations. Many persevered, however.

Twelve members of this immigrant's family lived in a three-story walk-up. Only four of them had jobs. In order to keep those jobs, they had to work overtime—without overtime pay—or "rat" on their friends in the factory. But this woman feels lucky. She never snitched. When the hard times were over, she could feel proud that she had kept her honor.

World War II

Although I was too young to go to war, I knew that the situation was bad because those who returned from overseas never really talked about it. In addition to the war's price tag of untold billions of dollars, the toll in terms of lives and psychological injuries was staggering.

In time, the survivors rebuilt their lives. Some got married and had large families. Some bought small homes made afford-able through Veterans Administration loans. Some took advan-tage of the GI Bill; instead of coming home to blue-collar jobs, they were able to go to college. They had a taste of what only rich kids had tasted before. This group of first-generation college men went on to become lawyers, medical doctors, corporate executives, and writers.

Sputnik

The day the Russians sent the *Sputnik* capsule into orbit and beat the Americans in the space war was a dark day in American his-tory. No longer regarded as the unchallenged scientific and tech-nological leader, the country began to worry that it might not be able to compete with the Russians in other areas.

Our concern affected every aspect of society. Educators, criticized for not emphasizing science and math, were mandated to change their school curriculums. Money was poured into the space program.

From those dark days came the programs that put Ameri-cans on the moon. The technological advances led to the subse-quent launch of the *Vanguard* satellites, the astronaut program, and the *Apollo* missions. These helped provide a myriad bene-fits: the hand-held calculator, the microwave oven, the computer chip, and the solar-charged battery. From *Sputnik* we learned that a punch in the stomach could do us good.

The 1960s

For anyone over thirty, the 1960s were hard times—times of questioning, of disrespect from young people, of feeling that it wasn't OK to be just an ordinary person. The assassinations of John and Robert Kennedy and Martin Luther King Jr., and the beginnings of antiwar sentiment that swept the nation, characterized the political unrest that threatened to rip at the very fabric of our government.

While the younger generation was occupied with sex, drugs, rock and roll, and "flower power," the marriages of many of their elders began to break up. Careers were abandoned. People no longer were sure about what they'd been taught to believe. Yet from those dark days we learned to stand up for our values.

Watergate

During the Eisenhower years, we believed our government was good. Didn't we overcome evil in World War II? Then came the sixties and, shortly afterward, Watergate.

The June 1972 break-in at the Democratic National Committee headquarters in the Watergate office building—and the cover-up by the Nixon administration that followed—changed the face of American politics forever. We learned that White House corruption and tyranny of grand proportions were possible even in a democracy. Our distrust of government increased, and if government was bad, what else was bad? Could we ever trust any institution again?

From those hard times came the loss of what was left of our innocence about our leaders. That was a good thing. We're more realistic now. We don't automatically trust anyone. We're less willing to believe in campaign promises and more able to evaluate our leaders' performances. We're more demanding in the qualities we feel a good leader should have.

Downsizing

In the 1990s we saw our buddies lose their jobs and fail to find new ones. Global competition had changed the game. There would be no more jobs for life, no more pensions to count on, no more big benefits or reasonable fees for our medical insurance. We never knew when we would get that tap on the shoulder signaling we had lost our job. As modern-day industry and technology began moving at a more rapid pace than ever before, we struggled to keep up. Sometimes this meant learning new skills and starting all over. Sometimes it meant an early retirement and feeling that we no longer belonged in the workplace.

As we realize that our workplace is no longer a secure environment, we're turning our attention to the things that matter. We're enjoying our families more. We're exploring our spiritual nature. We're taking care of our health. We're adapting to hard times in a world that never stops changing.

> **Anticipating hard times helps us prepare for—and survive—them.**

Bringing Out the Best

Hard times bring out the best in us. As Moses learned, in times of hardship the need for leadership is amplified. When the Pharaoh punished the Israelites for requesting a sojourn in the desert to pray to their Lord, Moses was confused. He didn't understand why, in spite of his following the Lord's instructions, further hardship should befall the Israelites. Moses knew that stronger leadership was required. He went directly to the Lord, who helped him enact plans for bringing hardships to the Egyptian people—from the royal court to the lowliest peasants—in order to soften the Pharaoh's heart.

Today it's up to our leaders in business and politics to know when to turn up the volume on their leadership skills.

- In the wake of the fatal shootings at Columbine High School in Colorado, the leaders of the Justice Department and the Federal Trade Commission joined forces to investigate video-game and other entertainment companies who market violent fare to children. Responding to the growing speculation that such games and other media contribute to teenage violence, these organizations began exploring the role of advertising and other profit-making ventures in influencing the behavior of children.

- In his push for greater equality for minorities, civil rights leader Jesse Jackson has sought to bring more diversity to Wall Street. Raising hundreds of thousands of dollars to support his Rainbow/Push Wall Street Project, Jackson has put the pressure on Wall Street to recognize minority-owned firms as credible financial institutions.

- As commander-in-chief of the country's military forces, President Clinton led the successful, though drawn-out, NATO air-strike bombing of Yugoslavia. Although no one anticipated the level of defiance that Yugoslavian President Slobodan Milosevic would demonstrate, Clinton's resolve never wavered. As the air strike dragged on, with both civilians and Serbian soldiers suffering casualties—including the mistaken bombing of the Chinese embassy in Belgrade—Clinton persevered. His determination, and that of the NATO leaders, paved the way for overriding Milosevic's program of ethnic cleansing.

- During the Watergate crisis, *Washington Post* reporters Bob Woodward and Carl Bernstein exposed the Nixon administration's criminal conduct. Through their investigation, America's leaders and the public learned the full extent of Nixon's cover-up attempts. Their journalistic leadership role played a significant part in uncovering the activities of top officials and in Nixon's resignation.

A Time of Testing

In every society are rites of passage, or tests. They are the way society sorts out those who are the children and those who are the adults; those who are the leaders and those who are the followers.

Moses' Tests

One story has it that before the Lord selected Moses to be a leader, he put a sheep in Moses' path. The sheep wandered off. Moses took responsibility for bringing it back. When Moses realized the sheep was thirsty, he told the sheep that had he known this earlier, he would have carried the sheep to the stream. In this story, Moses passed the test. He had the compassion and the sense of responsibility for effective leadership.

Once he became leader of the Israelites, of course, the tests became tougher. When the Lord hardened the heart of the Pharaoh against the Hebrews, Moses was frustrated. But he had faith in the Lord and went to the Pharaoh repeatedly to request that the Pharaoh let his people go. While Moses was pleading with the Pharaoh, he had to keep the Israelites' spirits up. "But they hearkened not unto Moses for anguish of spirit, and for cruel bondage" (Exod. 6:9). Moses had his hands full. But these tests prepared him to deal with the Israelites' rebellious ways in the desert.

The Lord constantly tested Moses, even up to the time of his death. Before he died, Moses spoke to the Chosen People. He told them that Joshua would be their new leader. He selflessly meditated on the nature of human existence, pointing out to the people how transitory it was compared with other things that the Lord had created—the mountains, the earth, the sky. Moses also reassured the people that his death would in no way weaken them. He told them to trust in the Lord and Joshua. He blessed all the tribes.

Moses then hiked to the top of Mount Nebo and looked across to the Promised Land, which he would never reach. Never once did he reflect on what he did not have, or pity himself because he had failed to reach his goal. Moses had passed the test: he had learned that in the journey came the teaching; with achievement came the reward.

Before he went up to Mount Nebo to die, however, Moses warned his followers about the many arduous times that awaited them. It was the final teaching he would ever share with them, and he saved it for last, perhaps because of its importance. The Lord had told Moses that the Israelites would not remain strong. He predicted their downfall and the tragic consequences of their failure to follow the Lord's teachings: "Behold, thou shalt sleep with thy fathers; and this people will rise up, and go a-whoring after the gods of the strangers of the land, whither they go to be among them, and will forsake me, and break my covenant which I have made with them. Then my anger shall be kindled against them in that day, and I will forsake them, and I will hide my face from them, and they shall be devoured, and many evils and troubles shall befall them; so that they will say in that day, 'Are not these evils come upon us, because our God is not among us?' And I will surely hide my face in that day for all the evils which

they shall have wrought, in that they are turned unto other gods"
(Deut. 31:16–18).

Moses shared the Lord's words with his people. As a true
leader, he had done his best to prepare his followers for the hard
times that lay ahead. It is a lesson that every corporate executive
might heed in looking toward the day when the going gets
rough.

In Our Time

Our world is global, information driven, and uncertain. Many of
us who expected a quiet, predictable life are running into plenty
of hard times. Maybe we're forty-seven years old with two children to put through college, and we lose our job. Maybe our
mate decides to marry someone else. Maybe at work new soft-
ware has been installed and we still haven't learned it. Maybe our
house plummets in value.

Whether we like it or not, whether or not it's fair, many of
us must learn how to navigate through rough waters. Those of us
who succeed will become the new role models for younger people. Not too long ago the people we were taught to admire were
those who stuck with something. Maybe it was a lawyer who
wasn't crazy about the law but stayed at his firm for thirty years.
Or the corporate executive who wanted to buy a bed-and-break-
fast but stayed in the marketing department until retirement. Or
the immigrant from India who sold newspapers and magazines
whether there was rain or snow.

Today we admire men and women who can bounce back
from hard times, and, if necessary, change.

- A public relations executive who made about one million dollars a year lost his job. The man hunkered
  down. He cut his expenses. He reached out for emotional support from friends and family. Soon he had

landed another prestigious job. Now that man's a hero for our times.

- In the late 1980s, a Stamford, Connecticut, woman invested her life savings to buy a condo. In the mid-1990s, the condo plummeted in value. The woman became scared. She wanted to abandon the condo. Instead she took a meditation class and joined a gym. She held on to the condo until it recovered all its value. By persevering, this woman landed on her feet.

- In Stephen R. Covey's *Living the 7 Habits,* Pete Beaudrault recounts how a heart attack led to a major life change. A "company man," he quit his stressful job to become chief operating officer of Hard Rock Café, where he helped develop a company that has been responsive to such employee issues as working hours, benefits, and bonuses. He has said, "The restaurant business can grind people up, so we try to help our employees build their self-worth and their sense of belonging to a larger community. It's good for them and it is good for the company and believe me, I know it is good for me, too."

As a popular saying goes, when the going gets tough, the tough get going. There's a certain type of person who excels in these times.

- Prime Minister Winston Churchill led England during one of that country's most difficult times. During World War II, with his inspiring rhetoric, he not only turned around domestic opinion favoring Neville Chamberlain's policy of appeasing Hitler, but also engaged the United States' support in protecting England from the Nazi threat. Recognizing the peril that lay ahead for his country, he understood the necessity for action.

- As head of Mattel Inc.'s Barbie doll line in the 1980s, Jill Barad helped the company recover from near bankruptcy and brought it to a leading position in the toy industry. By the late 1990s, however, the company faced declining sales and stagnating stock prices. As Mattel struggled to keep its edge, Barad, now CEO, rallied to add a new chapter to the company's success story. Emphasizing global expansion, new technology, diversification, and entry into e-commerce, Barad embraced the hard times. "When it comes to strategic underpinning and what is broken and what needs to be fixed, those are the challenges that I love. I love looking for the holes," she has said.

How many of our sports superstars have toughed it out, played the game, and won? Such heroic performances have inspired entire teams and brought the teams' efforts to a higher level.

Tips for Leading in Hard Times

Just as Moses was a leader through the hard times, so can we. In fact, it's easier to do the incredible in hard times than in normal times. Here are some tips.

✔ Drop the Humility—Sometimes

Moses' humility was ill timed when the Lord commanded him to become a leader. Despite promises from the Lord that the Lord would be with him every step of the way, Moses still backed away. This was a hard time for Moses. He was unsure of his abilities. The Lord was angry with him. Moses realized that he had to replace his humble nature with a leap of faith in order to accept the mission.

✔ Explain the Hard Times

One of the most difficult things for a leader to do is to explain to his or her followers why bad things happen. Moses didn't duck this responsibility. When enemies attacked or loved ones died, he communicated his belief in a divine plan. Many leaders are called on to put the hard times into a perspective that their followers will understand and accept.

✔ Accept Your Fears

We all look to our leaders for strength. But that doesn't mean our leaders don't share our fears, or have their own. While he was participating in the Lord's miracle of parting the Red Sea, Moses was scared. Some executives suffer from "performance fright" before giving a presentation. Successful leaders do not give in to their fear, but rather turn it into a positive force. They learn to say hello to their fear in the morning and good-bye to it at night, and not let it interfere with the rest of their day.

✔ Take Responsibility

Realize that people are depending on you. Most likely there were many times that Moses would have liked to turn and run away, but he didn't. He knew the people were relying on him for their physical, emotional, and spiritual survival. The fact that other people are dependent on us helps to lift us out of ourselves and into a higher place. It is there that we become our best selves. Whether we're entrusted with a pet, a child, a classroom, or a nation, we're motivated to think about someone other than ourselves.

✓ **Turn to Something Bigger**
During hard times it's useful to have something or someone bigger than ourselves to turn to. Moses frequently turned to the Lord. It was this belief in a supreme being that allowed him to get through the ordeals of leadership.

✓ **Take the Test**
The curve balls that life pitches at us are tests. They're opportunities for us to prove who we are to others and to our own selves. There was a time when our office lost a few accounts. The loss was unexpected. The company's leaders regarded the situation as a test of our strength: Could we make it through lean times? We did. After that we were prepared for anything.

If it weren't for the hard times, many of us still would be emotional babies. Much of our learning and growth—as people, parents, educators, leaders—has come when we faced difficulties and navigated our way through them. By embracing hard times, we embrace wisdom, courage, and power.

**Hard times present
both leaders
and followers with
new opportunities.**

9

No Spin Doctors

> **M**. *Scott Peck opens his inspirational best-selling book* The Road Less Traveled *with a basic truth: "Life is difficult." Although he could have written some spin about how wonderful life is, or how easy it is for us to make our lives better, Peck chose to tell the truth.*
>
> *Millions and millions of people have been helped by Peck's philosophy. Many recovery groups recommend his book to their members for their meditation sessions. While other inspirational leaders have come and gone, Peck has lasted for more than two decades. The truth has staying power.*

We live in a world of spin doctors, those elusive technicians of language who twist the truth into shapes that change its structure, yet give it enough familiarity to make it believable.

Spin sells, but only if we buy it. Spinning the truth is an act of desperation, often to gain or regain control.

- As the eleven-week air war by NATO forces against Yugoslavia ended, President Slobodan Milosevic agreed to the withdrawal of Serbian soldiers from Kosovo and the repatriation of thousands of refugees. The Serbian leader tried to put a positive spin on his defeat, calling his failed war effort "a great achievement." Backing away from a position of weakness, Milosevic heralded the end of the war in a televised speech, proclaiming, "Today our sovereignty is guaranteed."

- Defense attorney Johnnie Cochran proved to be a master spinner. Aiming to direct the attention of the jurors of the O. J. Simpson trial away from damaging DNA evidence that linked Simpson to the murders of ex-wife Nicole Brown Simpson and her friend Ronald Goldman, Cochran made accusations of racism against his client's prosecutors and won a controversial "not guilty" jury verdict.

- How many spins have we heard from our leaders on controversial issues? Has the United States administration claimed that China has improved its human rights agenda in order to keep trade going between the two countries? Has Russia's President Boris Yeltsin passed off his health problems stemming from alcoholism and heart disease as mere cold or flu symptoms in order to keep up his image as a strong and viable leader?

Spin doctoring happens outside the political arena. Individuals in business and the professions have sought to gain by hiding the truth.

- As an entrepreneur, Paul Edward Hindelang Jr. was legendary. He had built a modest pay-telephone business, Pacific Coin, into one of the country's largest independent pay-phone operators. While he was negotiating a long-distance deal, he was forced to admit to a truth he thought would never come to light: in the 1970s, he had served time in prison for smuggling marijuana. When the truth was made public, Hindelang lost his position as CEO.

- Kim Stacy, a columnist for Kentucky's *Owensboro Messenger-Inquirer,* wrote a story about her travails with terminal brain cancer. In fact, Stacy had contracted AIDS and had decided to cover up her illness by attributing her condition to a more socially acceptable disease. Because of her deception, she was fired from the newspaper.

The Truth Be Told

In this information age, we're all becoming more sophisticated about what is and what isn't spin. At one time politicians could mesmerize people with their eloquent words, but no longer. Today we can read their faces and body language on television. We can go online to Web sites like drudge.com and salon.com and learn how others are challenging what they say. We can follow the reporting of traditional print media, television, and radio journalists who are trying to get beyond the spin and uncover the real story. Today we are less willing to take things at face value and more willing to push truth as the value of choice.

Our leaders are beginning to get the message. They are learning from the mistakes of the past. Political leaders such as George W. Bush Jr. have tried to become more plain-speaking. Senator Bill Bradley has always tried to play it straight with the American public.

In business, our leaders are beginning to understand the value of speaking the truth, no matter how painful.

- Dr. Jerry MacAfee, chairman of Gulf Oil Co. until his death in 1991, led the petroleum producer through one of its darkest chapters—involvement in a foreign bribe scandal. As the company's new CEO, MacAfee would not compromise the truth. He forbade his speechwriters to mention any book he hadn't read or any movie he hadn't seen. By setting a personal example, MacAfee helped reestablish Gulf Oil's reputation.

- During the downsizing at the former NYNEX, vice president Doug Mello explained to employees exactly how the company's reengineering would take place. Not all of it was pretty, but Mello respected his people enough not to give them false hope. He realized how easy it would have been for workers to think their jobs were not in danger.

- James Burke, chairman of Johnson & Johnson, faced a public relations nightmare when seven people in the Chicago area were poisoned by Tylenol capsules that had been laced with potassium cyanide. Burke went on national television, condemning the individual responsible for the death of a twenty-three-year-old woman who died after ingesting a tainted capsule.

Rather than trying to deny or minimize the company's responsibility to protect consumers, Burke announced a plan to end the production of all capsule products and replace them with caplets. "Since we can't control random tampering with capsules after they leave our plant, we feel we owe it to consumers to remove capsules from the market," he said.

Truth telling among individuals is equally powerful, building trust and creating bonds.

- A colleague of mine once called me and admitted she was no longer doing well in public relations. She was convinced that her career in communications was finished. I listened to her admission. The fact that she told the truth made me care about her, and I told her that she was probably right. The field of communications likely was not right for her any longer. Our candid conversation helped this woman to leave the industry. She went on to become a top-producing financial planner. Had either of us been evasive, this woman still might be floundering.

- Ivan Seidenberg, CEO of Bell Atlantic, told the truth to a prospective employee he was interviewing for one of his former employers. "You're bright, funny, and wrong" for the company, he told her. The woman agreed and withdrew her application. By being truthful, Seidenberg prevented a potentially unhappy relationship between the company and the applicant.

- A CEO once confessed to me that he was having a lot of trouble with his company's board of directors. They wanted him to make changes that he didn't want to make. He asked my advice. I honored his track record for success. I praised him. Then I explained how past success can make us apprehensive about changing the formula. Within a few months this man was more in tune with the board. He had heard the truth and was able to accept it.

Like Moses, our leaders don't have to be spin doctors. They can tell the truth and still inspire people.

And Nothing But the Truth

Moses knew the value of telling the truth. This required a lot of courage. The Israelites were a hot-headed lot. Frequently they doubted that the Lord would take care of them, and just as often they rebelled. Having witnessed their temper tantrums, Moses didn't massage the truth. He consistently presented things as they were, even when the people threatened to stone him. Often he was afraid for his life because of it. "And Moses cried unto the Lord, saying, What shall I do unto this people? They be almost ready to stone me" (Exod. 17:4).

An extraordinary leader like Moses will put his life on the line in the pursuit of truth.

The Truth Behind the Law

The rules that governed the Israelites came down from the Lord in bits and pieces. This meant that Moses was frequently explaining to the Chosen People what the Lord expected from them. He had a tough job because some of the concepts he had to communicate were complex.

For example, Moses explained that justice didn't always mean retribution. The Chosen People, in fact, were instructed sometimes to help their enemy. "If thou meet thine enemy's ox or his ass going astray, thou shalt surely bring it back to him again" (Exod. 23:4). Here Moses is touching on a very sophisticated psychological truism: Hate will destroy the hater. The Israelites probably weren't thrilled to hear this. Faced daily with survival, their reflexes were to strike out at their enemy. Because most of the Lord's concepts constituted a new way of thinking and living, Moses had to keep explaining God's truths until they sunk in.

The Lord also provided highly detailed instructions on how to build the tabernacle, the Holy of Holies. He covered every base, from the materials that should be used to the exact dimensions. While building a place of worship was important, nothing was more important than observing the Sabbath, the day of rest. No one was to work on anything on the Sabbath, not even the building of the Holy of Holies. Moses made explicit what other leaders leave implicit. He left nothing to chance or interpretation. Telling the truth meant telling all of what lay behind the Lord's laws, even those the Hebrews did not understand.

Many of today's leaders don't like to get bogged down in details. They're too impatient. They wrongly assume that their followers should somehow intuitively know what has to be done and how. Then when the followers don't deliver what is expected, they're punished.

Telling the Truth to the Lord

Moses also had the courage to speak what he saw as the truth to the Lord. Once the Lord became very angry at the Israelites and wanted to destroy them. Moses presented a truth to the Lord. He pointed out that it was the Lord who had led the Chosen People into the desert, in view of all of Egypt. If the Israelites were to die in the desert, the Egyptians would have, one might say, the last laugh. The Lord spared the Israelites.

Time and again, this leader pleaded for his people. He was always persuasive with the Lord, but he didn't try to manipulate the facts with either God or his Chosen People.

Creating an Identity

Like most leaders, Moses used the truth to help his followers develop a particular identity. Because the Hebrews had been slaves for centuries, they had a specific mind-set. For instance, they did not see themselves as being different from the Egyptians in many important ways. A small minority of them are thought to have worshiped, as the Egyptians did, bulls, crocodiles, cats, and even snakes. Moses had to educate the Israelites that their Lord was an elevated deity who alone ruled the world. There were to be no other gods before the one God of Israel.

Today's leaders around the world are also helping their followers maintain or establish their identity. In our global marketplace, many workers are finding themselves owned or influenced by foreign companies. This means that their identity as a citizen of the world must be cultivated. Yet they also are citizens of their own countries and are proud to maintain the customs and rituals of their people. Striking a balance will be a challenge to these employees and their leaders.

Many companies try to allow their international workers to maintain separate identities. This plan often backfires. Boutique investment banking partnership Lazard Frères & Company decided to integrate its three operations in London, Paris, and New York. Accustomed to stressing their individualism, the operations fell behind other, more fluid global banking networks. Other company leaders believe there is no longer any room for a territorial approach that seeks to maintain the differences among countries in employment practices, such as salaries and pensions.

Seeking worldwide cooperation is not an easy task. Leaders must learn to speak the truth about an integrated economy and tone down the nationalistic rhetoric. That is a hard message to communicate. The leaders of Italy or Germany, for example, no longer can speak solely in terms of what's good for their countries. Forging a new identity for citizens in a "borderless world" will be one of the major challenges in the twenty-first century.

Effective leadership means searching for the truth while embracing the "big picture."

Teaching the Truth

It was also Moses' job to help his followers understand why things happened the way they happened. Sometimes these lessons were difficult to learn.

When Moses' brother, Aaron, was being ordained as High Priest, his sons, Nadab and Abihu, deviated from the usual rituals and offered sacrifices that were not approved by Moses and not acceptable to the Lord. The Lord punished Nadab and Abihu. Because they were priests, they were struck dead for not following the letter of the law.

It fell to Moses to tell the Israelites what had befallen the two young men. He also had to tell Aaron the truth behind the tragedy and to explain what was to be learned from it.

Spinning Out of Control

What is the truth? Is it a legal construct? Is it what people believe it to be? Is it what can be divulged only at a certain time in history?

The world will always have people who manipulate the truth for their own purposes—whether it's the leaders of communism, who claimed that all people would become equal, or President Saddam Hussein of Iraq, who called the United States the "Great Satan" in order to arouse his followers.

And there will always be countries whose leaders try to alter their role in history. So-called revisionist historians, for example, claim that the Holocaust never happened. Japanese publishers canceled the publication in their country of Iris Chang's *The Rape of Nanking*, a history of the atrocities committed by Japanese troops against the Chinese in 1937, after Chang purportedly refused to make changes in her book.

Will our leaders be able to discern the truth as our histories unfold?

To be prepared to speak the truth means that you are prepared to hear it.

Guidelines for Truth Telling

Telling the truth doesn't mean we have to tell every overweight person that he is fat, or advise a cancer patient that she may have very little time left to live. Telling the truth requires experience and compassion. Medical doctors and psychologists must learn how to tell the truth to patients. Even old hands at management sometimes find it difficult to bring bad news to employees. Frequently they seek counsel with a human resources consultant or a mentor before addressing their staff. But all of us can become better truth tellers. Here are some guidelines.

✓ **Put Yourself in the Other Person's Shoes**
By doing so, we'll know better what to say and do.

✓ **Ask Yourself, "What Would Abraham Lincoln Do?"**
Lincoln had enormous respect for people. He never underestimated them and always felt they deserved the truth. If we treat others with honor, the truth will come out just fine.

✓ **Put Your Truth to the "Giggles Test"**
Before I talk to employees about their performance, I try out in my mind how the talk would go over with my teenage son. If I imagine that my son would start giggling, I change what I had planned to say.

✓ **Try to Avoid Giving Pain to Others**
The truth doesn't have to be brutal. Most managers know they can explain to employees that they might fit better elsewhere rather than use a "Get out of here, you dead wood" approach.

Avoiding the Spin

Hundreds of times a day, the world tries to manipulate us. It's our responsibility to protect ourselves from the spinners. Here are some tips.

✓ **Ask Yourself: "What Do I Really Want?"**

The doctor tells us that if we don't lose weight, we're going to die prematurely. Obviously he's trying to get us to control our food intake. He may be exaggerating. Regardless, the question is: What do we want? Do we want to live with the risks that being overweight entail, or are we willing to change our eating habits? Perhaps the boss tells us that everyone in the department has an MBA. Of course, she's strongly hinting that we also should get an MBA. Do we want that, or should we consider other positions for which an MBA won't be required?

✓ **Examine the Motivations of Others**

My ninety-something mother might tell me that I need a new suit because she may not like the one I am wearing. The salesperson at Brooks Brothers might tell me the same thing because he wants to make a sale. If we assess other people's motivations, we'll be less susceptible to manipulation.

✓ **Realize That There Are Very Few Emergencies**

We have time to decide what we want to do. We can ask the telemarketer to call back next week. We can ask the client if we can have a few days to think about it. We can ask our children to wait just a bit.

✓ **Don't Try to Please Everyone**

We've all been socialized to try to give people what they want. If they want to see us happy, we smile. If they want to see us frustrated, we act agitated. Actually, it isn't all that hard to say no. There are many ways to say it. We can refuse to get on someone else's wavelength. We don't have to give everyone what they expect from us. We don't have to be constantly manipulated.

Tell the truth at
all times.
There is no substitute.
Moses, if he were
alive today,
surely would agree.

Summary

Through his actions and words, Moses has shown us that it's possible to be a great leader. It was not easy to behave as Moses did in biblical times. It took enormous courage and true faith.

Life in the twenty-first century is far more complicated. The global economy, diversity, technological know-how—these are only some of the challenges faced by today's leaders.

Today, men and women are beginning to take more control of their investments, their communication, and how they obtain knowledge. Many will be called upon to be leaders and will need to develop the necessary core strengths. These would-be leaders can benefit from Moses' lessons in leadership.

Be Selfless

Moses believed in something bigger than himself. He was able to transcend the ordinary and become great. By believing in something bigger than ourselves, we can grow beyond our limitations and reach immeasurable heights.

Be a Follower

Moses was a great leader and a flexible follower. When we follow someone else—the boss, the athletic coach, the head of the school board—we forget our own desires and focus on what the leader wants.

When we're leading others, we think of what's best for our followers.

✓ **Be Humble**

Moses knew when the burdens of leadership were too heavy for him and asked for help. Today no leader can do everything. Ask for help, structure a winning team, and offer support—the reward will be the involvement of others who, in turn, will reinforce, redirect, and recharge our leadership skills.

✓ **Practice Self-control**

When Moses indulged his emotions, there were consequences. Today we're working too much, eating too much, complaining too much about what we don't have, and demanding too much from our leaders. A return to moderation might be just what we need.

✓ **Give Thanks**

Moses recognized the importance of thanking the Lord for help and taught his people how to follow his example. Learning to feel and express gratitude is the foundation of a society. It's not hard to say thank you; the hard part is remembering to do it. A simple thank you is often enough to reinforce the task of followers: to support their leaders and accomplish their goals.

✓ **Show Compassion**

Moses was able to balance the letter of the law with the spirit of forgiveness. Countless times, he went to the Lord and asked for mercy for the rebellious Israelites. In today's litigious society, opening our hearts to those who have done wrong will make our decisions more humane. There is wisdom in forgiveness.

✓ **Learn Effective Criticism**

Moses knew how to correct his people's behavior without breaking their spirit. Most criticism is ineffective because it's delivered in the wrong way. Give guidance constructively and with empathy.

✓ **Embrace Hard Times**

Moses knew nothing but hard times. He learned how to solve problems during crises. By focusing on others rather than himself, he clearly identified the problem. As leaders, we can function better in hard times if we concentrate on the situation at hand. If we rise above the circumstance, like Moses did, we can achieve the perspective we need.

✓ **Tell the Truth**

Moses didn't spin. He told the truth exactly as he saw it. That's how he was able to earn the Israelites' trust, secure their willingness to follow, and remain a leader among an angry, resentful people. Telling the truth builds trust and creates powerful bonds.

Moses wished nothing more than to have his followers join him in his mission. Like him, today's leaders need to develop effective ways of reaching their followers.

The demands of the new millennium on our leaders will be significant. Mastering new technologies, working out mergers, making accurate decisions, and forming concrete game plans will be essential to the success of our corporations, our government, and our families. The wise leader will view this not only as a challenge, but also an opportunity.

Like Moses, today's leaders must rise above their egos. Moses wasn't great despite his modesty, he was great through it. Emulating Moses is our key to successful leadership.

About the Author

Robert L. Dilenschneider is founder of The Dilenschneider Group, a corporate strategic counseling and public relations firm based in New York. He was formerly president and CEO of Hill & Knowlton, Inc., where he worked for nearly twenty-five years.

From major corporations and professional groups to trade associations and educational institutes, his experience covers a wide variety of fields and includes dealing with regulatory agencies, labor unions, consumer groups, and minorities, among others. He has lectured before numerous professional organizations and colleges, including the University of Notre Dame, Ohio State University, New York University, and the Harvard Business School.

Mr. Dilenschneider is a member of the advisory boards of The Center for Strategic and International Studies, New York Presbyterian Hospital, the College of Business Administration at the University of Notre Dame, and the North American Advisory Board of The Michael Smurfit School of Business at University College, Dublin. He is also a member of the board of directors of "Prep for Prep," a New York leadership development organization that finds jobs each summer for over two hundred students; a trustee of the Institute of International Education; and a former member of the Board of Governors of the American Red Cross.

He is a member of the Council of Foreign Relations, the U.S.-Japan Business Council, the Economic Clubs of New York and Chicago, and the Florida Council of 100. In recognition of his contribution in promoting New York City, he received the city's "Big Apple" award. He is also a member of the Public Relations Society and the International Public Relations Association.

Mr. Dilenschneider is widely published, having authored the best-selling *Power and Influence, A Briefing for Leaders, On Power, The Critical 14 Years of Your Professional Life,* and the forthcoming *Corporate Communications Bible.*